"I have learned to travel with only wh[...]

—Suzanne de Passe, executive producer, *Lonesome Dove*

"In a world of distracting, stress-inflicting audio, visual, informational, and physical bombardment from which few of us are immune, I've spent most of my student and professional life in some form of 'conflict resolution.' Physical and personal places of peace and renewal are invaluable to me. Regina's practices create a calmer personal center. From this flows a strength leading to greater work and personal performance. If you practice even some of these precepts, you will find that they work, as I have."

—Brian Walton, lawyer, consultant, professional negotiator, and former executive director of the Writers Guild of America and Chief Negotiator for the Screen Actors Guild (2001)

"I knew having Regina organize my home would make my life easier and make me feel better. I didn't realize that was just a small part of what was taking place. She opened up my life and living space for the right things to come in. This is something that continues to happen every day! Regina taught me that clutter in your home translates itself into your life. For that, I am eternally grateful."

—Monica Vonneumann, television host

"The Best Organizer in Los Angeles"

—*L.A. Magazine*, July 2001

"Thank you, Regina, for teaching me how to tame the endless sea of papers in my office!"

—Rupert Maconick, producer, Salville Productions, Los Angeles

"A fantastic organizing book …. It helped me, and I have it here somewhere!"

—Elayne Boosler, comedienne

the

ZEN

of

ORGANIZING

the

ZEN

of

ORGANIZING

by
Regina Leeds

ALPHA
A Pearson Education Company

Publisher: Marie Butler-Knight
Product Manager: Phil Kitchel
Managing Editor: Jennifer Chisholm
Acquisitions Editor: Mike Sanders
Senior Production Editor: Christy Wagner
Copy Editor: Michael Brumitt
Cover Designer: Doug Wilkins
Book Designer: Karen Ruggles
Creative Director: Robin Lasek
Indexer: Angie Bess
Layout/Proofreading: Svetlana Dominguez, Gloria Schurick
Marketing and Publicity: Dawn Werk, 317-581-3722

*"For everything
there is a season,
a time for every matter
under heaven."*

—*Ecclesiastes 3:1*

This book is dedicated to the late Kay Jones—therapist, teacher, and friend.

Contents

Foreword   xv

Preface   xix

Introduction   xxiii

Acknowledgements   xxxi

*Journey of discovery: How an actress became the Zen organizer.
(The story of the grunions.)*

1   **Getting Started**   2

Where do you begin?
*The "whole" of anything is overwhelming. We must learn how to
break our tasks into small, manageable segments.*

What preparations are in order?
*We need to honor the reality of our physical body and to respect
the wishes of those with whom we share the environment we seek
to change.*

How much time do you allocate?
*Rome was not built in a day. Neither will the chaotic patterns of
a lifetime yield in a matter of minutes.*

How do you make this effort different from all past attempts?
*Perhaps Socrates said "the unexamined life is not worth living"
after the tenth time he tried to clean out his closets! It takes more
than wishful thinking or good thoughts to change. It requires
understanding and the conscious redirection of our energies.*

Why is this work more difficult for you than for others?
*There are specific obstacles to success in this arena. Once iden-
tified, the equally specific cures can be implemented.*

2   **Time**   14

*Matching the reality of our lives to our goals. (Crafting the
life pie.)*

3   The Work Space   38
    Why the home office is frequently doomed to failure (the story
    of the therapist with receipts in her underwear drawer) and
    the drama of the traditional office (the story of the boss who
    could and the secretary who refused).

4   Closets   68
    Matching the inner and the outer you. (The story of the di-
    vorced actress.)

5   Bathrooms   80
    A fresh start for a new day. (The story of the earthquake couple.)

6   Kitchens   96
    Nurturing the soul's vehicle. (Meet the professional cook with
    the bare cupboards.)

7   The Common Rooms   114
    Learning to care for others through our shared spaces. (Meet
    the New Jersey cowboy.)

8   Children's Rooms   136
    From cradle through raging hormones: Teaching a life skill.
    (Meet the kind actor who played bad guys.)

9   Physical and Emotional Ties to Chaos   148
    Unexpected challenges, unexpected cures.

10 Maintenance and Reality   164
    Surrounded by piles again? There's a reason and a cure.

11 Benediction   184
    How to bless the newly organized home with Feng Shui.

12 Frequently Asked Questions   200
    Everything you ever wanted to know ... about being
    organized ...

    Index   233

Spiritual Energy

Foreword

My introduction to Regina Leeds came in a roundabout, seemingly haphazard manner. Knowing I was entertaining the idea of making some changes in my home environment, a casual acquaintance suggested I work with Feng Shui master Nate Batoon. It felt spontaneous and daring to call and schedule time for a practice about which I know very little, but upon meeting Nate I intuitively knew the work would be of great significance to me and my life. In the few short hours we spent together in my apartment, Nate and I focused on my primary goal of finding and moving into a new house. In order to achieve this goal, however, I had to do some cleaning out and reorganizing of my existing space. It was, for some vague reason, an extremely daunting task and not one I felt I could do alone. Perhaps one of Nate's most precious offerings to me that day was in scribbling down Regina's name and phone number, sharing his knowledge of what would soon become a most exquisite resource for me.

"Of sentimental nature and an artistic temperament" is a diplomatic way to describe me and the subtle chaos of my personal space when I first met Regina. My closets were filled to capacity, piles of books and papers perched respectably in standing sculpture form throughout my apartment, and cupboards and drawers were random and screwy in their attempt to store my household necessities. In other words, my home was a mess, and I knew it. What I did not know was where to start to restructure my systems of organization and how to create the efficiency I longed for. As much as I hold on to the belief that life is inherently chaotic, I also hold the competing belief in and desire for order. Add to that a restless readiness to change, and there you have me, overwhelmed, opening the door to invite Regina into my life.

There is a palpable grace and calm energy that emanates from Regina like a warm glowing sun. She is clear, direct, and present. Her integrity and style are evident immediately, as is her ability. What she establishes with her clients up front, however, is that she is not a fairy godmother come to wave a wand and make messes magically disappear. Her intention is to guide, assist, and teach her clients how to maximize the flow and function of their physical space, thereby maximizing their very basic human potential. Hers is a deeper purpose, as you will discover in reading this book.

The process of working with Regina may begin practically with the cleaning out of a closet or a desk. What quickly becomes apparent, however, is the larger meditative action of space being made internally as well. With the help of Regina's objectivity and creative solutions, I not only made room in my closet; I made room in my heart and mind. In the six months since I began to work with Regina and implement the methods she puts forth in this book, great changes have occurred in my life. Most notably, I made a move from an apartment to a house. With the help of her ideas and her good care, this transition has been creative and fun. She has blessed my life, as I hope you will allow her to bless yours.

Annebeth Gish, actress

精

Essence

Preface

*"I'm not here to convert people,
I think it's better
to keep your own tradition ...
Everybody has the potential
to make a contribution
to human development."*

—*The Dalai Lama*

I began using the phrase "Zen organizing" several years before I actually sat down and wrote this book. Although I am not a serious student of Zen, I deeply admire its precepts and am drawn to its simplicity. You do not have to become a Zen practitioner in order to profit from this book. The Zen of organizing refers to the creation, in your home or work area, of a calm, peace-filled, joyous environment. Zen organizing will benefit you, no matter what spiritual path you have chosen to walk.

I recognize a Zen-organized environment the minute I enter one. It's the *feel* of the room, not just its *appearance*. If you follow the guidelines in this book, you, too, will experience what it means to be Zen organized. Alone in an office that invites your best efforts, cooking in a kitchen that seems to hand you the tools you need, or falling asleep in a restful bedroom, you will suddenly smile and say to yourself, "Oh, *this* is what she was talking about."

When we finish a project, my clients always marvel at what we have accomplished together. Inevitably, the call to perform one simple task like setting up a new file system has been unexpectedly accompanied by shifting the furniture in the room or cleaning out *all* the cupboards and drawers. As one area is brought into harmony, the surrounding itself seems to call out for attention. It is as if the very room and the things in it *want* to be Zen organized!

Zen, itself, is not a religion; it is a practice. I wish to bring three aspects of Zen to your attention:

- The first is "beginner's mind." Just as it sounds, it is bringing to your spiritual practice a mind free of pre-conceived notions and judgements.

- The second aspect of Zen is concentration on the breath. It might be said that a true practitioner lives from breath to breath.

- Finally, there is the aspect of mindfulness. I like to think of mindfulness as being *truly* conscious. Have you ever driven down a road and suddenly wondered how you arrived at this point in the journey? Your mind wandered from the task of driving. You were on "automatic pilot" and were not driving mindfully.

Each organizing challenge requires the same things: the openness of beginner's mind, focused concentration, and a mindful approach. As a Zen organizer, here's how I work:

- I calm my clients when we meet. We consciously leave fear and judgement behind. The absence of this destructive duo places us in beginner's mind. Now we can tackle the project and not be hampered by extraneous inner dialogue that frequently sounds something like this: "I can't get organized because I don't have the organizing gene" or "I'll never be able to do this!"

- ❧ We stay focused in the present moment quietly establishing order one step at a time, just as the Zen practitioner focuses on one breath at a time. The meat of the process is this ability to make one decision at a time.

- ❧ It's hard to think clearly and make good decisions when we are not working mindfully. Most Westerners have only a piece of their consciousness anchored in the present. Another part of the mind is busy rehashing the past, while still another part longs for the imagined perfection of the future. You're trying to file your business receipts against an inner cacophony of words: "Why did he do that to me when I was only a child?" ricochets around your inner world, causing you pain. The next minute, the equally powerful "I know I will be happy when I … (marry John or Mary, win the lottery, or move to Paris)" ricochets back. You need not be a victim of your thoughts. The past and the future should be entertained only when invited, just like your in-laws! And it doesn't take a Zen master to accomplish this feat.

As you read these words now, they may not make much sense. "What is she talking about?" you think to yourself. After reading this book and getting one or two projects under your experience belt, you'll re-read this Preface and think, "Of course, I know *exactly* what she's talking about." In the not too distant future, you, too, will *live* a Zen-organized life.

始

Beginning

Introduction

> *"Nature demands change*
> *in order that we may advance.*
> *When the change comes,*
> *we should welcome it*
> *with a smile on the lips*
> *and a song in the heart."*
>
> —*Ernest Holmes*

In the summer of 1979 while making a completely forgettable film called *The Fish That Saved Pittsburgh,* comedian Jonathan Winters gave me a piece of advice that would alter the course of my life. "I'm crazy, Reggie," he said, "but I make a million dollars a year because of it." Jonathan told me to make my neuroses pay. I gave that a lot of thought over the years. I had enough neuroses for 12 years of therapy. Never once, no matter how hard I tried, was I able to isolate a neurosis that anyone would pay me to exercise.

Solving the Riddle

Composer friends told me they heard music everywhere. Dancers told me they heard rhythm in the sounds of everyday life. Photographers and painters saw images worthy of capturing forever. I saw the order inherent in every bit of chaos I observed. It wasn't a conscious effort on my part. Untamed stacks of papers in offices caught my eye. Cupboards in the homes of friends would open to reveal a jumble of unrelated things. I would fix it all in my mind wondering why they had never thought of the various solutions that occurred to me. Almost 10 years after meeting Jonathan, it finally dawned on me that this was the neurosis people would pay me to exercise.

The riddle was solved.

The Roads Converge

I asked a friend who was unorganized if I could help her put her home in order. Being organized was one thing; communicating how I achieved it would be new territory. As is frequently the case, many roads converged in this endeavor.

I am an only child. Today my mother would be considered a hip woman who had postponed motherhood until her thirty-seventh year. In the Brooklyn of my youth, she was an oddity: an "old" mom. She was so self-conscious that I never played with other children. My mother was sure she would be judged by their mothers. When I was five years old and taken to my first day of school, I suffered a deep trauma when Sister Charles Veronica opened the door of the classroom to reveal a room full of children. I had quite honestly never seen so many people my age and size. I understood how to deal with adults, but this was foreign territory. Wasn't everyone at least 40 years old and 5'4"?

You see, in my isolated world, I had learned to play alone. In fact, one of my favorite activities was rearranging my toy chest. Every week my mother, who was reading nearby, would hear the unmistakable sounds of the lid of my toy chest being propped open and boxes being lined up on the floor around me. "What are you doing, Sweetheart?" she would ask, as if she did not know the answer. I told her I was arranging my toys so it would be easier to play with them. "But you just did that last week!" she would say, her voice communicating a clear "Are you nuts, child?" "I know, Mommy," I answered politely, "but I can't play with them unless the boxes are edge to edge." To her everlasting credit, my mother let me perform this ritual that she so clearly viewed as an exercise in futility.

My mother instilled in me the need to be orderly. I have never thrown clothes on the floor or left dishes stacked in the sink. Had I done so in my mother's house, even as an adult, her sizeable Lebanese hand would have whacked my bottom soundly. Interestingly, my mother was driven by a different set of needs than I was when it came to our personal environment. My mother was the classic depression child: by nature a pack rat and overly concerned with what other people thought about her. The parts of our house that you could see were absolutely perfect.

However, the inner structure was in chaos. I was appalled by the state of my mother's closets and drawers. "What difference does it make?" she would say. "No one can see the mess." This is where we parted philosophical company. I never saw a difference between the inner and the outer environments. I wanted everything in order because it made me feel calmer. Work was easier to accomplish in this ordered universe. Filing for me wasn't a problem because I set the files up to yield their treasures and absorb additional information. Getting dressed was a creative adventure because all my clothes were neatly organized in one area. In my mother's "perfect to behold" bedroom, clothes lived in chaos. They were thrown into dresser drawers or jammed into her closet. You get the picture.

I went to college and received a degree. I could count on one hand the number of teachers who had a profound influence on my intellectual development. One such teacher was Professor Vera Roberts.

One day Dr. Roberts gave us an impromptu lecture on the true value of our education. Even though the system was set up to teach us in isolated classes, we could connect the dots. What, for example, was going on in France while Columbus was discovering America? Simultaneous with these developments, what were the contemporary views of mathematics and science? "All knowledge is one," she said. That one statement changed my thinking forever.

Later, I learned there were other disciplines based on this unifying theory. In Chinese medicine, for example, the body is treated as a whole. The doctor of Oriental medicine is not a specialist in one particular part of the body. He traces all problems back to their root. As a professional organizer, I view the entire space as one unified whole that is capable of influencing our ability to function. When a client has a messy office, I know that the closet is a disaster. When the kitchen is in chaos, I know that the bathroom cupboards are a war zone.

The Story of the Grunions

Grunions are small fish who appear once a year off California beaches. It is possible to catch them in containers the way children back East might capture fireflies in a jar. Many years ago a friend of mine told me this story. "When I was 18, I took a girl to my high school prom in my father's brand-new Cadillac. After the prom, my date wanted to go to the beach and capture grunions. Like any dutiful 18-year-old boy, I took her and we quickly scored a bag full of the tiny fish. We tucked the treasure into the glove compartment of my father's car. There were several stops before the night ended and you can guess what happened. The grunions were forgotten. Within two weeks, the unmistakable stench of dead fish emanated from the glove compartment. Needless to say, my father almost killed me!"

Now what does this have to do with your piles of papers or your messy closet? Everything! My friend is a therapist and uses this story to illustrate the importance of dealing with our emotional issues. "If you don't," he says, "they'll fester like the unseen, rotting fish and have a profound effect on your life." **Piles of messy clothes and stacks of untended papers will swirl their chaotic energy around you like an evil spell.** It will be difficult to think clearly. You will feel mildly depressed when you're in your home or work environment. It will be hard to work there whether your task is washing dishes or drafting contracts.

My clients frequently ask if organized people aren't simply born that way. I assure them that while some of us are born with an eye for order and an inner need to have everything in place, **everyone can learn how to organize their lives.** We all know someone who plays the piano by ear. Does it follow that a desire to learn how to play the piano should be abandoned if one was not born with this gift? I think not.

And so the little girl who had to organize her toys before she could play with them, and who wondered why the inner life of a house was not as important as the parts on display, became a professional organizer who teaches people how to achieve the Zen of an organized space.

The Role of Spirit

I was raised in a Catholic church that has vanished from Brooklyn. The Mass was celebrated in Latin and the schools were run by nuns in full regalia. In fact, my high school was staffed by five different orders of nuns! We were taught that God had sent us here with a specific vocation. There would be unavoidable consequences to the soul if you did not heed this call. Unfortunately, the prospect of eternal damnation was sometimes less frightening than the earthly punishment doled out by the nuns if they did not approve of your declared vocation.

My parents wanted me to be a doctor, a lawyer, a teacher, or a nurse. The nuns sent home notes suggesting I enter the convent. As you might imagine, the isolated, only child surprised everyone with her chosen profession. No list had actress on it except mine and, I presumed, God's.

I majored in drama at Hunter College and pursued acting and singing with the dedication of an evangelist. No one could stop me from what I was convinced was God's will for my life. You may have seen me in national commercials for your favorite products. Perhaps I made you laugh on your favorite sitcoms. Some of you would remember me on *The Young and the Restless,* where I recurred for three years. As the age of 40 came in site on the horizon, and with it the knowledge that good roles for women would become scarce and finances tighter, I decided to start my own business. When I realized that organizing would be the vehicle, I was delighted as it gave me an opportunity to enrich people's lives, something I had always hoped my performing did as well.

Acting made it easier to speak in front of groups when I started to teach my class. It also made it easier to delve into the psyches of my clients and understand why they had problems being organized. I had, after all, spent my adult life trying to understand the characters I was hired to play. Those roads were converging again, as if I had been led to this moment during a journey I had assumed would end in a different way.

I left the Catholic Church at 17, ever grateful for a superior education and a quest for God that would color my adult life. The years that followed found me in search of a spiritual home. I stayed for over 10 years in the Church of Religious Science founded by Ernest Holmes. My studies here took me to the brink of becoming a minister. I loved their psychological approach to life and the importance of self-responsibility. My work in therapy dovetailed with the work I was covering in classes at church. I presumed the better I understood myself, the better I would be at understanding and creating believable characters in my acting. Little did I know how different I would be asked to apply this knowledge. One day, I looked at the circumstances of my life and realized that the path I had been seeking had long been beckoning to me. I embraced the spiritual teachings of yoga.

To the average Westerner, yoga is a series of pretzel-like poses meant to be an alternative exercise to aerobics. Very few realize that the postures are actually one tool in a vast and ancient spiritual philosophy. Most consoling of all for me is the yoga concept of doing what the soul has come here to express. *The words changed in every path I examined, but the message is the same: You have come here for a reason.*

My clients have come from all walks of life. I have worked with doctors, lawyers, homemakers, actors, producers, writers, and salesmen. The outer circumstances were immaterial, like clothing to be changed. Each was in transition in his or her life, and I recognized myself as a human catalyst for change. *The calm environment we would create together would support their daily lives. This ease in living would help them accomplish that for which they had been sent. It is no different for you.*

Of course, you may not believe in a higher power. The amazing feature about organization is that it allows one to be in control of one's environment. This in turn lends itself to control over one's life. We live in a cause-and-effect universe, and as we consciously change the causes we set in motion, the more desired effects result. And this yields power.

I have yet to meet any honest human being for whom the words "power" and "control" are not a form of aphrodisiac. They can be used to gain mastery over the temptations of life that form an impediment to one's quest for God, or they can help you run for political office. It is certainly not my place to judge. This book has, therefore, been written with two groups of people in mind: those who believe in God and those who do not.

Acknowledgments

*"I thank my God
every time I remember you,
constantly praying with joy
... for all of you."*

—*Philippians 1:3–4*

The night of the Academy Awards every actor worth his salt runs to the bathroom during the commercial breaks to rehearse his acceptance speech. If he has any dignity, the speech usually stresses the fact that creative endeavors like a film are really team efforts and he has a lot of people to thank. I spent most of my life as an actor, dreaming about this big moment. This acknowledgements section is, in a way, my Academy Awards speech.

The transition from actor to writer was a difficult one. At one time I thought Zen organizing was a consolation prize. I believed the only thing that mattered was success as an actor. It isn't every day that what you originally perceive as a consolation prize turns out to be the gift of a lifetime. My first thank you is, therefore, to God.

Three extraordinary teachers graced my life and changed it forever. Ardelle Quinto taught me to sing. Guru Ramakrishna Ananda introduced me to Eastern philosophy and the path of yoga. Feng Shui master Nate Batoon taught me the spiritual ramifications of the organizing work I did for my clients.

My heartfelt thanks to Udana Power, Steve Mathis, and Ann Slichter for being the first to encourage me to write a book. They saw the possibilities long before I did. In fact, Ann so believed in this project, she edited the original manuscript.

I want to thank my dear friend Debbie Zoller, who had the courage to be my first paying client. Debbie is a professional makeup artist in the entertainment industry. I'm honored to say that the same hands that have worked on famous faces like Patricia Arquette, Mel Gibson, and Jimmy Smits did the makeup for the photographs of me you see in this book.

All the clients who followed have been my teachers. Without their trust and honesty, I would never have understood what material a book like this should include. They brought me their areas of challenge and together we created order from chaos. It is not easy to ask a stranger for help in changing patterns that no longer serve us. I salute and thank all of them.

When people told me writing a book was easy compared with the task of getting it published, I didn't believe them. Ignorance is indeed bliss. A writer works in solitude. It takes a village to birth a book. My village happens to be populated by a group of extraordinarily kind, generous, and talented people.

Captain of my team is my best friend, Susie Ribnik. Susie's official capacity was desktop publisher of the original manuscript. Later she worked as the editor for all material that was written or revised after I lost Ann Slichter to a lucrative TV job. Susie is my business mentor and head cheerleader. Many people played key roles in this process. Susie is the only one who stayed from start to finish. I can never adequately express my thanks.

Anne Taylor urged me to write magazine articles. Joy Davidson generously taught me how. Patti Britton introduced me to iVillage and instantly gave "Zen organizing" an audience of eight million. The tireless duo at Casa Graphics, Patty and Ernie Weckbaugh, created the look of the self-published version of *Zen* that preceded the one you are holding in your hands.

When I decided to add Chinese characters to the manuscript, Dr. Linda Zhang graciously drew them. Randy Madden donated his computer skills to keep me up and running through all the various stages of this book. The incomparable Corinne Edwards invited me to be on her show, *Books on Tour*. Later she encouraged me to meet her agents. I am forever in her debt. Marilyn Allen is everything you dream about in a literary agent: talented, hard-working, and ethical. She not only secured a deal for *Zen;* she did it in record time.

I offer special thanks to Mike Sanders and the entire team at Pearson Education/Alpha Books. No writer has ever been treated with more respect. Mike understood *Zen* from the beginning and worked tirelessly to have it published, asking for my input at every juncture. I am forever in his debt.

The book you are holding has been blessed by all the people mentioned here who contributed, each in a unique way, to the process. If I have accidentally left out the name of someone who helped, I extend my apologies. The omission is just that … an accident.

I am honored to dedicate *The Zen of Organizing* to the late Kay Jones, my therapist and friend. I hope that wherever she is, Kay knows about this book and is proud of me. I have no words to express the void her death has left in my life.

Finally, this book came into being with the daily help of a very special friend. Indeed, she sat with me during every writing session and offered her encouragement. She is my friend and companion, my muse, and perhaps the child I never had. She is Katie, the world's greatest Golden Retriever.

Grace

CHAPTER 1

Getting Started

"Shifts in taste and perception
frequently accompany shifts in identity.
One of the dearest signals that something
healthy is afoot is the impulse to weed out,
sort through and discard old clothes,
papers, and belongings.
By tossing out the old and unworkable,
we make way for the new and suitable.
When the search-and-discard impulse seizes you,
two crosscurrents are at work:
the old you is leaving and grieving,
while the new you celebrates and grows strong."

—Julia Cameron in The Artist's Way

I remember vividly as a child my mother cleaning before the housekeeper arrived so she wouldn't think ill of us. It made no sense to me. When a new client calls to make an appointment, I ask them not to touch a thing in their home or office. As a professional organizer, my role is to help, not to judge. I assure everyone that the more complex the situation, the more fun we'll have solving the problems of the space, and besides, no one is ever half as complicated as they imagine.

Brain Dance

This does not mean, however, that I am never overwhelmed. When a large home, for example, is to be put in order and chaos reigns, the energy in the space can produce what I call "brain dance": the inability to think clearly or deal with the situation at hand. When this happens, I remind myself to practice what I preach. You see, *the whole of anything is overwhelming.* The way to bring peace to a chaotic environment is to break the task down into small manageable increments. The old phrase about Rome not being built in a day holds great truth. You can only clear off your desk by deciding the fate of one piece of paper at a time. Your closet will only yield to order if you deal with one article of clothing at a time.

Because each human being and every situation is different, it is not possible to declare that the kitchen, for example, is the first place to start. I try and read the client's emotional state to see just how ready they are for change. I also try to decide which area will have the greatest impact on the environment as a whole. It's a funny thing about order, but it starts to spread like a fungus. My clients experience how order makes them feel calm while chaos jumbles their nerves.

Nothing is as restful to the eye first thing in the morning as a closet, for example, that has its contents arranged by type and color. Finding the outfit you wanted to wear that day is a snap because there is only one place for it to be located. Is it missing? You will be reminded that it has been taken to the laundry or the cleaners.

How many of you begin the day with a series of small irritations that send you out into the world expecting things to go wrong? Your closet, to continue with our example, is designed to hold your clothing. It was never intended to be an early morning battlefield. It not only yields its contents in a helpful manner, but it can be visually calming and easy to maintain. Your entire house can be designed this way, including your kitchen, where I hope you prepare a healthy breakfast; the bathroom, where you clean and prepare your body for presentation to the world; and even your car, which transports you to your destination. My clients inevitably get what I call "the fever": the desire to put the entire home or office in order ASAP.

So where should you start? If you have any confusion in your mind, please take a moment to answer the following questions:

- **Is there an area that "frightens" me?** Let's say you want to organize your closet and your desk. You can never find what you want to wear and your desk surface disappeared years ago. If success in business is how you identify yourself, your desk will not be the easiest place to begin. I would ask that you go into your closet and start clearing out old clothes. You will be developing what I call the "trash muscle," that is, the ability to easily part with "stuff."

  And you will be gathering together items that can be donated to a charity where they will have a new life with someone less fortunate. As most charities will give you a donation slip for your income tax, this is definitely a win-win situation. (By the way, be sure you get your donated items out of the house as you make your decisions. I learned long ago I had to take the donated items to the charity or else they would magically migrate back into the closet as I was pulling out of the driveway!)

- **Will I have a block of at least five uninterrupted hours?** You did not create the current situation in five minutes. You won't be able to restore order in that amount of time either. No matter where you start, you will find an emotional charge with every item you touch. The internal critical parent will be asking you, how did you let this happen? Why do you imagine you can succeed? *If you try to work in fits and starts, you will convince yourself of failure.*

If you are serious about changes in the environment, get a baby-sitter, let the answering machine or your secretary pick up your calls, and don't answer the doorbell or respond to that knock on your office door.

First-time clients very often balk at the prospect of spending five hours with me on our first session, so I make them a deal. If we examine the project and it can be accomplished in less than five hours, then I will not charge them for the extra time. In all these years, I have yet to come across the short initial project. It does not exist. Honor your commitment to change and allow the time necessary to make permanent changes in your life. There is no rush to completely alter everything at once. In fact, when done in manageable increments, the work can be more enjoyable and permanent.

❧ **Remember that it gets worse before it gets better.** There is always a moment when my clients look around the room and I can see panic wash over their faces. I sense them thinking, "Does this woman know what she's doing?" I tell them to stay calm and to trust that it's about to come together. I use the analogy of birth: Labor is painful, but the end result is worth a little suffering.

❧ **Consider the schedules and the feelings of those good folks with whom you share your environment.** Let's say, for example, that you are a stay-at-home parent who wants to have a kitchen worthy of Martha Stewart. If you tear the cupboards apart on a Saturday morning while teenagers and their friends are running in and out, you will not only frustrate their efforts to eat, but you will endanger the success of the project.

Once you begin altering the environment, it can be enormously threatening to the other individuals who live or work there. So while you are in quest of the perfect place to begin honing your organizing skills, think about the emotional and physical needs of the people sharing your environment. Getting organized is a way to make life easier; it is not a secret weapon in the "relationship wars."

Let's imagine for a moment that the initial task has been chosen. In subsequent chapters as we work in detail on the various project areas in a house or office, we will note the things you'll probably need to purchase. You wouldn't want to spread your papers all around your home office in tidy stacks only to realize two hours before your family returns that you forgot to buy manila folders! The physical space will make its demands. There is another physical set of demands we must honor in order to ensure success. These are the demands not usually acknowledged as being a part of the process:

- **You live in a body. It needs nourishment in order to function at maximum potential.** Before my students show up for class, I ask them to eat a good breakfast and bring healthy snacks to class (think a glass of orange juice or a slice of cheese rather than a candy bar or buttered popcorn). I would urge you to have some bottled water at hand and to indulge often: It's a great antidote to stress.

- **Acknowledge whether you are a morning or an evening person and schedule accordingly.** Most of my clients like me to arrive first thing in the morning. When I work on my own projects, I start midday and work into the night. This work is difficult physically, mentally, and emotionally. Give yourself the edge by working when your body's natural rhythms will support the process at hand.

- **Wear comfortable clothing.** I think I have shocked a few clients who expected me to show up for work in a red power suit and high heels. I like to sit on the floor or feel free to crawl into the upper reaches of a closet. Blue jeans and a casual shirt are appropriate for this kind of work. Leave the pearls for a night at the theater.

The Endless Loop

When people get the organizing fever, they generally want to share their excitement with others. If you just can't contain yourself, you may start to hear comments like these: "Oh, that's great, honey, but the real trick is keeping it organized." "You'll never be organized. People in our family just don't have that gene." "I'll believe it when I see it."

It is also possible that these voices will not belong to those who know and love you or even those who simply share your business environment. These comments may be playing on an endless loop inside your own head. I want you to deal with these fears before you start.

Please take a moment to ask yourself the following questions:

- What is my ultimate goal? (What will being organized help me to achieve?)
- Have I ever tried getting organized before? How is this time in my life different? And how will this difference impact my current efforts?

- Have I carefully chosen my initial project?
- Did I make all necessary preparations in order to ensure success?

We live in a cause and effect universe. The chaos you are now living in, you have created. Every time you throw another piece of paper into a pile, you are creating that chaotic setup as if you enjoyed the results. It is amazing how loyal people can be to systems that destroy their ability to work effectively. *You can now shift your mental, emotional, and physical worlds to create a reality that supports your goals, rather than one that makes achieving success an additional obstacle course.*

I believe you can make your work in the physical world that much more powerful by incorporating *creative visualization.* You have the opportunity to see your new reality in your mind's eye before you bring it into the physical world. Teenage girls enjoy imagining what a special date will be like. Young professionals picture an important business meeting. Pregnant women try to imagine their delivery. A young jock will envision a big play on the football field. You get the idea. In other words, creative visualization may sound exotic and foreign to you until you realize you've been doing it all your life.

Unfortunately, we tend to picture the worst outcome and live in fear of it becoming a reality. "I just knew it!" someone screams, as the wrong road is taken on a trip or something is discovered lost or stolen. Again we are confronted with the reality that, to a great extent, we do create the world we live in. Jesus said: "It shall be done unto you according to your word." Let's set a few good words into motion in the world.

I invite you to exercise your imagination by doing the following:

- See life as you want it to be.
- Picture yourself working easily and quickly to carry out the tasks necessary to bring this change into existence.
- Imagine yourself enjoying what you accomplish.
- See clearly how your new circumstances benefit others in your life.

Celebrate the chaotic world that you have created!

It brought you the experiences you needed up to this point in time. *As the architect of this chaos, you are all powerful in your personal environment.* Come with me now on the adventure of creating peace.

The Magic Formula

Let us suppose that absolutely everything is in place. You stand before your chosen area with all the tools you'll need, a bottle of water, and a full tummy. *There are three steps you will follow to achieve success in your project. These are the same three steps you will apply to any project you undertake in the realm of getting organized.* You can clean out a closet, organize a desk, or plan a wedding following these guidelines. We will apply this formula in every chapter. *Here is your introduction to the magic formula:*

- **Eliminate.** Remember when we acknowledged the whole of any project as being overwhelming? After you isolate the starting point, you can gain further control by eliminating from the area what you absolutely do not need. On a desk, this is the paper that is no longer relevant to your work. In a closet, it is the articles of clothing you know in your heart must be bagged for charity.

❧ **Categorize.** As you toss the unwanted, the items that are to remain start to fall into identifiable groups. You'll find papers related to that house sale you negotiated last year, or to the sport you're investigating in order to get back in shape. You'll want to put all of your related clothing items together. I like to color-code as well. (We'll discuss this in detail in the appropriate chapters.)

❧ **Organize.** Now, in lieu of mounds of chaos, you have identified the clothes you want to keep, the papers you'll need, the items for your trip, the food in the cupboard, and so on. We will investigate creative ways to put these related items into their new home. Any system we choose must do the following: Be restful to the eye, support the inherent function, and be easy to maintain.

I can imagine that some of you are wondering why it has been so difficult for you personally to succeed in getting organized. After all, we haven't been discussing rocket science. Everything has hopefully made sense and a lot of it you have probably tried in the past.

Consider This Scenario for a Moment

You wake up one morning and your bedroom is filled with people furiously tearing through your things. They have uniforms on and are packing your suitcases for a trip. Someone notices that you are awake and they pounce on you with hearty congratulations. You have been chosen to represent the United States in an Olympic event! Unfortunately, it is a sport you have never heard of, much less tried. You are panic stricken, but your visitors assure you that you will be fine. Off you fly to some exotic foreign city where you promptly make a fool of yourself in your event. "I'm sorry," you explain to the U.S. press. "No one ever taught me how to do it."

Guess what? *Getting/staying organized is a skill, and if you aren't very good at it,* I'm going to guess there was no one around to teach you. It's that simple. And just like a sport, there are levels of accomplishment. The only thing that matters is that you expend the time and energy to reach your full potential.

At this point, you have a choice. You may want to speed-read the entire book before getting started, or you may want to do your preparation and "meet me" in the chapter that covers the initial challenge you want to face. Either way, I know you will succeed. When you go to a yoga class, you are shown a posture and told to replicate it to the best of your personal ability. If Gumby is teaching the class, you might be intimidated! A good yoga instructor, however, will assure you that you will receive all the benefits of the posture even if you are so stiff your bending forward stops at a whisper of an incline. So, too, whatever you achieve is a magnificent step forward in my estimation. We all begin at a different starting point. And the finish line is equally calibrated to our individual abilities.

Let the Games Begin!

平

衡

Balance

CHAPTER 2

Time

*"Lost time
is never
found again."*

—*Ben Franklin*

Your life is created by the way you use your time. The vast majority of people do not plan their path through life. Day-to-day activities and emergencies impact them and carry them from one hour to the next. The hours become days, the days turn into weeks, the weeks dissolve into months, and so on. These undirected humans are buffeted by time and its demands as if they had no say in the matter. Their passage through life reminds me of the graceful descent of autumn leaves to the ground. Leaves have no goal or target. The wind decides their fate. It is a poetic but meaningless journey. Periodically, someone will wake up from this self-imposed trance and wonder why his or her dreams have not been achieved. Anger, sorrow, and disappointment will reign for a few days and then the *dance of denial* continues.

The Substance of Life

In this chapter, I have written exercises for you to do. I promise you that these simple exercises will give you great insight into the way your life is currently unfolding. *I want to empower you so that you are in control rather than a victim of circumstances.* If time is not your area of challenge, I invite you to do the work anyway. At the end of this chapter, I'll show you how to modify the exercises for application in other areas of your personal universe. You might just be surprised by what you discover about yourself if you do write out the time exercises.

Creating the Canvas

Please take three minutes to write in the following space exactly why you want to get organized. Be specific and brief. For example, the stated goal of "I want to get organized" is too broad. We have acknowledged the "whole" as being overwhelming. Let us focus on an isolated area of challenge so that our chances for success are increased. Here is a list of things you may relate to:

- I can't find important papers when I need them.

- I miss appointments.

- I don't feel I have control of my day.

- I run out of household staples like toilet paper before I get to the market.

- I can never find what I want to wear in the morning, and so on.

Be sure and touch on how this challenge makes you feel. Does running out of toilet paper make you feel stupid? Are you ashamed when an appointment is missed or a bill is paid late? Does the drama of a lost paper annoy you? It is important to identify your challenges. It is equally vital you understand how they impact you emotionally. We touched on these concepts in the first chapter. Let's take a deeper look now and see what we discover. Writing out your response will help you pinpoint the root causes of your chaos. You might write something like this: "I want to get organized because I never pay my bills on time and this makes me feel like a failure."

I won't be coming by later to give you a grade, so if the mood strikes you to write more than the requested one sentence, remember what my mother used to say: "It's okay; nobody dies!" I want to help you change your life. I don't want to give you a new tool with which to shame yourself.

If you have a timer handy, set it now for three minutes and begin writing your response in the space provided:

I want to get organized because …

_____

_____

_____

_____

_____

_____

_____

_____

I am going to assume you have made previous attempts to work on this problem. Look at your current situation and contrast it with those other times in your life you tried to change. This is a key step in your ability to succeed. If you discover circumstances have actually worsened, it might be best to get control of the situation before you seek to change it, albeit for the better.

Let me tell you the story of a wonderful working wife and mother. Sheila called and booked me to organize her closets. She was in such a rush to get organized we actually started working together the day before a major holiday. She had an amazing freedom when it came to parting with possessions. For her, the next step was to take my class. I called Sheila a few weeks later just to see how she was doing.

Imagine my surprise when she told me that everything had returned to chaos. "I guess this organizing thing just isn't for me," she said despondently. I couldn't believe my ears. What had gone wrong, I wondered? How had she lost her momentum? It turned out that her two preschool children had come down with the flu and had been bedridden at home for over a week. This would throw a monkey wrench into anyone's schedule. And there was more. Their illnesses had coincided with her husband's emergency back surgery! The amazing thing about all of these emergency circumstances was that Sheila did not see how they were responsible for her dropping the organizing ball.

From my perspective, Sheila first needed to deal with the situation at hand. As soon as everyone was well, she could continue her journey of creating an organized household. **A clear assessment of the situation coupled with a desire to change and a commitment to the process will empower you beyond your wildest dreams.** Do we not encourage young children to learn from their mistakes? One day you were stymied by the task of tying your shoelaces. Today the frustrating task is how to manage your time. Be just as patient and gentle with yourself as you master this new skill.

Should you uncover the fact that there has never been a more auspicious time to attempt change, you will be empowering yourself with this knowledge. Perhaps you were unhappily married for many years and are now newly single and living in your own space. Perhaps all of your teenagers are away at college and your home is no longer "teen central" for the neighborhood. These would be important factors in determining why this effort will be different. Understand and embrace the improved circumstances.

Okay. Pick up that pen and take three minutes to write your answers in the space provided.

This attempt to get organized is different from all previous attempts because ...

The Life Pie

We all divide the pie of our lives into various segments. We have a work life. We have relationships. We may have an active spiritual life. Some of us engage in sports or go to the gym religiously. Your life is unique and your division of time will reflect this aspect. Let's take a look at an example of a life pie. Here's one that is a little out of balance.

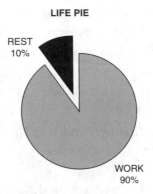

And here's one that's more balanced.

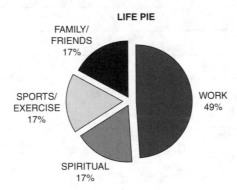

Let's take a look at your current life pie.

Take a minute to fill in this circle with today's demands on your time.

Please take five minutes and imagine, if you will, that you have successfully made the desired changes in your life due to an increased level of organization. How will your life be different in one year?

Indicate on the following blank pie chart what will be the important areas of your life and the time allotted to each area.

MY LIFE ONE YEAR FROM
TODAY PIE

Now you can describe the areas you indicated on the last pie chart on the previous page.

My life one year from today will be different in these respects ...

_____

_____

_____

_____

_____

_____

_____

_____

_____

Now I want you to create three lists. You may take two minutes to create each one or you can set your timer for six minutes and plug each thought into the appropriate column. Your worksheet model for this is shown in the following table.

The **first list** is what I lovingly term the **do-or-die list.** Here you indicate all the activities that you must perform without choice each week. Going to work to earn money is a solid bet for most people. If you have children at home, much of your time probably revolves around coordinating their schedules. If you are retired, I might find golf on your do-or-die list! Again, there is no right or wrong. I will not be sending you a grade, so feel free to be as open and creative as you are moved to be.

The **second list** is composed of **important tasks** that can be skipped without dire consequences. We might find house cleaning, laundry, grocery shopping, church or synagogue services, and cooking in this column. I like to do my chores on the same day each week. This routine gives me great comfort. If an emergency arises, however, and I must do two week's of laundry on the same night, well, you know, nobody dies!

Finally, we have a wish list. Here I invite you to jot down the things you hope to accomplish one day. Do you habitually promise that this is the year you will take an art class? What a perfect addition to the wish list!

Goals and Wishes

When you took the time to describe your life in detail in one year, you were honing your goal-creating skills. **Goals enable us to give our lives direction.** As we learn to set goals and accomplish them, we'll automatically be developing the ability to control our lives through the conscious direction of time.

The do-or-die list and the important list are the components of our goals. Think of building a bridge. First you develop the blueprint, then you work gradually and logically to create your new structure. As you become adept at breaking down your stated goals into the day-to-day components that will bring them into existence, you will be ready to consciously make time for the items on your wish list.

Have fun with this list!

The Do-or-Die List	The Secondary List	The Wish List
_____	_____	_____
_____	_____	_____
_____	_____	_____
_____	_____	_____
_____	_____	_____
_____	_____	_____
_____	_____	_____
_____	_____	_____
_____	_____	_____
_____	_____	_____

Now let's take a minute and write the previous items on the following calendar page. Like me, many of you work in professions where your weekly schedule fluctuates. Please just pretend this is a fairly normal week and don't be concerned that every aspect of every week cannot be contained in this space. This is just a microcosm of the whole, remember?

Monday	Tuesday	Wednesday	Thursday	Friday
———	———	———	———	———
———	———	———	———	———
———	———	———	———	———
———	———	———	———	———
———	———	———	———	———
———	———	———	———	———
———	———	———	———	———

Saturday	Sunday
———	———
———	———
———	———
———	———
———	———
———	———

Most of my students are shocked when they complete this exercise. Before them lie vast expanses of unused time they had no idea were available to them. Are you shocked to find that free time is available to you? You might, on the other hand, have so much activity written here that only a bionic person could possibly achieve any results. Either way, let's ask a series of questions designed to help us understand what this exercise teaches us:

   ❧ Is there any relationship between the life I am leading as indicated on my calendar page and the one I described I wanted to be living next year?

- Do I see how I am unconsciously draining my physical energy with all this activity?

- Is it safe to say I overbook myself?

- Is it time to delegate some of my tasks?

- Should I consider how cost-effective it would be to hire even a part-time helper?

- With your current schedule, will you ever realistically accomplish anything from your wish list?

- Am I avoiding something with all this frantic activity?

- Finally, we must ask ourselves the million-dollar question: How would I feel handing this schedule over to the person I love most and saying, "Here, you do this"?

Right about now, you probably need to take the dog out for a quick walk around the block. It's okay to take a break. How is your blood-sugar level? Would a piece of cheese or a glass of orange juice help? Seeing the reality of your life in black and white can be a little overwhelming. There is all too often a major disconnect between what we say we want and what we are actually doing on a daily basis. The task at hand is to bring everything we do into alignment with what we say we want. The phrase "Walk the walk and talk the talk" comes to mind.

Don't worry. I'm not going to abandon you now that I've uncovered your weak points. What was it I said before we started? Oh yes, the whole of anything is overwhelming! Let's examine each possibility here to see how we might solve the problem. You'll start to develop your own detective skills and will be able to solve any challenges I neglected to mention here.

The Reality of Our Goals and Our Schedules

New Year's resolutions are wonderful tools for change. They rarely work because what we want tends to remain in the realm of wishful thinking. This cause and effect world we live in can be altered with conscious effort. The person who wants to be 10 pounds lighter next year, for example, needs to find the right exercise program and alter his eating habits after he makes the mental commitment. Likewise, the person who wants to change professions may have to return to school or start sending out resumés after he decides his current situation is no longer satisfactory. Thought precedes action and change occurs naturally. *How can you alter your week to make your stated goals a reality?*

Draining Physical Energy

We live in physical bodies and must honor the systems in place to keep them in running order. I wish more than anyone that I did not have to eat, sleep, or exercise. I also am motivated and ambitious, and I want my body to transport me with ease and comfort for a long time so I "play by the rules."

If you own a car, you know that to keep it running at peak performance, you have a maintenance schedule to follow. In general, we take better care of mechanical equipment than we do our own bodies. Let's take a quick two minutes and write out some solutions to the problems you see indicated by the calendar exercise. For example, could you be eating more healthful foods? Do you need more sleep? Do some of these activities need to be eliminated? With a little thought and some courage to say no, you'll adjust things perfectly.

I could improve my schedule by ...

_____

_____

_____

_____

_____

_____

_____

_____

_____

There is also something I call *geographical intelligence*. One of my students discovered she went to the supermarket every day because she never made a list and was constantly running out of things. Add to the mix the facts that she is a single, working mom with three school-age children and she manages the apartment building she lives in. You can see why her unnecessary expenditure of energy was crucial. I suggested she make a shopping list and go to the store once a week.

For those of you who are computer-literate, there is a high-tech option. Take a few minutes to jot down every store you go to and the items you would be likely to purchase at each one. I go to one store for household staples like toilet paper and soap, but to a health foods store for food as I am a vegetarian and eat items not easily found at a general supermarket. Get the idea? Once you have the master list, you can put a copy each week on the refrigerator with a magnet. Every time a family member discovers that an item is about to run out, he or she must be responsible for checking it off on the list.

Let's look at a section of my personal list so you get the idea.

Supermarket	Health Food Store	Specialty Market
Toilet paper	Soy burgers	Cheeses
Tissues	Tofu dogs	Wheat-free waffles
Cleanser	Fruit	Wheat-free breads
Detergent	Potatoes	Chopped garlic
Dog biscuits	Sugar-free cookies	Juices
Ammonia	Sugar-free muffins	Snack foods
Sponges	Grains	Half and half

One final note in this area of geographical intelligence. When you look at your schedule, do you now realize that you tend to pick up your laundry on Friday before the weekend starts and do your food shopping on Monday to replenish the cupboards? Are the stores in the same part of town? Are they in the same shopping center? People will retrace their steps when one trip to a specific area is sufficient. Living in a car society, I try to conserve gas as well.

Overbooking

Let me tell you the story of the mom who couldn't say no. Marian is an old friend and a client of mine. She is a very successful business woman and the divorced mother of four school-age children. One day she booked me to help her unpack in her new home. This was an exciting time as she was moving from a tiny house they had long outgrown to a very large, roomy house in a lovely area.

The night before the big day, I decided to check with the movers I had recommended just to be sure all was in place.

Imagine my surprise when they informed me that the move had been postponed! When I called Marian, she apologized profusely for having forgotten to call me. You see, she felt she just had to say yes to two of the PTA committees at school, and that extra work had caused her to be unable to finish packing. Her inability to say no had created confusion in her schedule as well as for the movers and myself.

Don't be like good-hearted Marian. Honor your commitments with the time and respect they deserve. *No one can do it all.* An amazing truth emerges as we learn to say no: Nobody dies. If this is a life issue with you, you might benefit from reading some books on co-dependency. I used to suffer from this very problem. Now I enjoy saying no. Practice makes it easier over time.

Here's a tool to help you learn to say no. Have you ever noticed how happily married couples never agree to anything without saying they have to check with their spouse? No one is offended. We are probably taken with this level of commitment and respect.

Whether you are married or not, I want you to develop a personal relationship with your daily planner. *Never* agree to anything until you look at your schedule. I like the week-at-a-view or the month-at-a-view pages because I can gauge my willingness to add a task, do a favor, or make a social commitment by the fullness of my schedule around that time. For instance, if you call and say: "Regina, I'm having some people over next Thursday for a dinner party. Can you join us?" I'd check my book and see that I will be in the middle of unpacking an 8,000-square-foot home that week. I had better pass. My client needs my energy and I can't afford to squander it at a social engagement. I'd say something like, "Oh, gosh! I love your dinner parties, but I see in my calendar that I'll be doing a major unpack that week. I'm afraid I'll have to ask for a rain check. I never accept social engagements when I'm working on large projects." There are innumerable permutations I could use as examples here, but you get the idea. Sometimes you know instantly that you want to say no, but you can't muster the courage. Giving yourself the excuse of having to examine your day planner will give you time to formulate a polite regret.

Delegating

One day a perspective client got really angry with me when I suggested that delegating might be the solution to her super-busy schedule. "No," she said angrily, "delegating doesn't work. I tried it." I was fascinated and asked her to describe her experience for me. I was willing to be convinced.

She had joined a church when she moved into her new house near the ocean in Los Angeles. She was shocked that they had no materials ready to welcome new members and had formed a committee to create such a package. As she described her work, I was impressed by her creativity and attention to detail. Unfortunately, no one on her committee had come through for her and she found herself doing all the work. "You see," she said triumphantly, "delegation doesn't work."

Actually, delegating is a tool and it must be properly implemented. I told her she should have researched the background and investigated the schedules of the good folks on her committee. *It is important to ask the right person to help you with a task appropriate to his or her skill level and time availability.*

You also need to set "false goals." If I need you to report to me with information that I will work into a report due on Tuesday, I will give myself some leeway by asking for your information on Friday. Should you not be able to come through (especially likely in a volunteer situation), I will have created a few days of backup. One of us will secure what is needed and the final project will be completed on time.

Imagine, if you will, that the president of the United States holds a press conference tomorrow and announces that he is disbanding both the cabinet and the joint chiefs of staff. The reason? This president is sure no support is needed: He can do it all himself. Absurd, isn't it? It is no less absurd for you to burden yourself with the judgment that you are solely responsible for everything in your life. Martyrs in the Catholic Church were often elevated to saints. There are very few openings today in this field!

Hiring Help

For the person with financial means, this is not a big issue. For the rest of us, it can be difficult to imagine where even part-time, affordable help can be secured. I have some ideas for you to consider. Your local college or university probably has a job placement service.

If you run a small business out of your home, you might want to hire a student for a few hours a week to do the grunt work while you charge ahead with the creative side. You might even find someone in a major related to your field. The student will be earning money and getting practical experience.

Your local pastor, priest, or rabbi probably knows someone in the congregation who has retired but is itching to be involved a few hours a week in a business situation. You will be hard pressed to find a more devoted and knowledgeable person than a retiree.

I'm sure if you give it a few minutes thought, you'll come up with a creative solution to this matter. Somewhere out there is a person who can relieve you of stress and who will appreciate the opportunity to earn money. It's a win-win situation.

You just have to do a little work to make it happen. *Put your energy into the solution rather than into bemoaning the situation that is currently not supporting you.*

The Wish List

Take out your mental scalpel when it comes to the wish list. Eliminate what you know in your heart you are never going to do. Make a plan for the things you will feel deprived of if they are not accomplished.

Here's a letter-writing solution, by the way, that would curl my extremely proper mother's hair. Craft one letter on your computer and then adapt it to be appropriate for various people on your list. Use a font that looks very much like handwriting to help personalize its appearance. Too much trouble? Tell everyone to get e-mail!

Frantic Activity

One day a lady really needed to talk to me. She stayed during the class break and found me again after class ended. She wanted me to hear her schedule and be impressed with all she was able to accomplish. She told me she was completely unable to take a day for herself, but rather took an hour here and there. I sensed that being alone was not a comfortable experience. She needed to keep moving and to find her self-worth in the eyes of the large numbers of people she interacted with on a daily basis.

I wondered if there was any color in her face when all the makeup was removed. I noticed that her overly curled hair was a metaphor for her overly worked schedule. Obviously, she needed this activity, and it is not my job to make someone feel ashamed or wrong for the life choices they are making. My job is to open the door of possibilities and invite you to walk in and see if you'd be happier there.

I invite you to ask yourself why you are committed to so many activities and committees. Does your self-worth depend on the approval of others? Sometimes it isn't a chapter on time management but a few sessions with a good therapist that will set the stage for positive change. Don't be afraid to use all of the tools available to us in this age of communication.

The $64,000 Question

People are often surprised to hear me say that being organized is about 20 percent mechanics and 80 percent a reflection of self-love and self-esteem. If giving your schedule to someone dear to you would cause you discomfort, it's time to ask yourself why you are so demanding of your own time and energy.

Our schedules reflect to a great extent our views about the quality of life. Your schedule is a blueprint of your belief system. It may say things like, "I love myself and safeguard my energy." It can also reveal a personality that loves drama and fears change. You believe life is difficult, and you work hard to increase the level of difficulty. A schedule like this will sabotage you. I am suggesting you create one that supports you.

Other Applications

There is always at least one person in every class who does these exercises with great reluctance. They inform me at some point that they are very organized and just wanted to pick up some tips. Fair enough, I always think, because I too am always in quest of new ways to approach things. There are other applications for these exercises. Let's look at a few and then you decide what aspect of your life would benefit from being under the "written microscope."

Holiday Gift Planning

Every January you can hear the loud, anguished screams of credit card holders as their bloated monthly statements arrive announcing just how overboard they went during the holiday season. I want you to be the master of these details. I especially want your money to serve you. Let's consider how a little planning can help. Try the following exercise:

1. At the top right-hand corner of a blank piece of paper, please note the figure you would be comfortable spending over the holidays. If you do a lot of entertaining, let's make party planning a separate exercise. For our purposes, please list the gift-buying budget only.

2. Now make a list of all the good folks you feel you need to present with a gift. Leave about two inches between each name.

3. Go back to the top of the list and jot down next to each name one or two perfect gifts for this individual. Be creative. Some of you will say you never know what to buy and that's why you find yourself roaming the malls at the last minute. You would be surprised what you know about your friends and loved ones. For example, does your friend engage in a hobby? Is he going on a special trip this year? Does he tend to wear one color more than any other? If you are completely lacking any ability to observe, ask a mutual friend for help. You'll soon be known for the creative and thoughtful gifts you buy.

4. Note in the last column the amount of money you feel would be appropriate to spend no matter what the final gift is.

When you add the individually allotted amount, it will generally far exceed the figure you first noted in the upper right-hand corner. You will need to prune the list of some names and/or decrease the individual gift budget. For example, let's say your parents are about to celebrate their fortieth wedding anniversary and you know that they are dying to go on a cruise. You originally listed a cruise as the number-one gift you'd like to give them. A realistic appraisal of your finances won't allow this. Why not call the local YMCA or the Community Services Center of the local university or college and see if they have dance classes. You could present Mom and Dad with a gift certificate for some Latin dance classes with a sweet note saying this is in preparation for that cruise you want to send them on.

I can just hear some of you screaming, "Is she crazy? I can't do all that work!" If you would rather expend frantic energy running from mall to mall because that feels more normal to you, I won't stand in your way. It's always a matter of using energy in quiet-time planning or frantic-time shopping. If you are comforted by the latter, please just tuck the knowledge of another approach into your mental file called "Possibilities for Another Time."

The same exercise can be modified for myriad activities like party planning or business meetings. You can even plan your travel wardrobe long before you ever open a suitcase. I log what I am going to take on a trip about two weeks before I leave. I once caught a private van to a resort where I was to deliver the Friday night talk. I had my purse and an overnight bag. The Saturday night speaker had a large suitcase, a Pullman, and an overnight bag in addition to an enormous purse. She looked at my solitary bag and then down at her sea of luggage and said: "I guess I overpacked!" We broke out laughing and became instant friends. She told me later she just didn't want to forget anything. If she had made a list ahead of time, she would have felt more secure. And besides, we weren't teaching in the rainforest; New York tends to have whatever you need. I'll show you exactly how I plan for travel in Chapter 12, "Frequently Asked Questions."

In the meantime, let's take a look at a small holiday cocktail party plan following the preceding guide.

Guests	Budget: $1,500.00
Anne and Harry	
Susie and Jeremy	
Diane and Rick	
Jan and Doug	
Udana and Nate	
Helene and John	

Food Budget	$500.00
Liquor Budget	$650.00
Flowers	$350.00
Music	$300.00
Rentals (linens, etc.)	$200.00

It doesn't take a math genius to see that the individual elements of this gathering are quickly far exceeding my originally established budget. What to do? I can eliminate one of the following:

- One or more guests.
- Entertainment. (Forget the live harpist; let's play holiday CDs!)
- Switch to a less expensive caterer or alter the menu.

✤ Purchase one magnificent centerpiece and forgo the idea of flowers all over the house; use candles and scatter containers of potpourri around to enhance the mood as flowers would.

Do you get the idea? Instead of creating every element as I go along based on the whim of the moment, I can carefully craft and control the elements. As an actor, I learned to see all social functions as mini-plays. Be a wise producer and shop around for the elements that will produce the results you want and keep you in line with your finances.

Final Note

Select a regular time to *review* the plans for the upcoming week. For me, this will be either Friday evening or sometime on Sunday depending on my weekend work schedule. *Plan* your time in accordance with your long-range goals and with respect for your body, mind, and emotional energies. Let us teach our children by our example so that they will grow up living the principles we have struggled so long to master. We have been given the great gift of freedom of choice. Let us make good use of our time, and the creation of a productive life will be the gift we give our Creator in return.

Happiness

CHAPTER 3

The Work Space

*"… because there is only one of you
in all time,
this expression is unique.
If you block it (the life force),
fit will never exist through
any other medium and be lost."*

—*Martha Graham*

I returned from my first season of summer stock determined to take some dance classes. Following even the simplest choreography was beyond me. Acting and singing came easily; dancing was a horse of a different color. You have heard the expression "two left feet"? I had 12 left feet rapidly in motion once the music started. A dear friend, who was a professional dancer, suggested a school in New York and told me to start with the basics class. Being a trusting soul, I didn't ask any questions. I signed up for the minimum 10 sessions and showed up the first night. I wondered why I needed a basics class instead of a beginners class. I was sure, however, my friend knew best.

Learning from Humiliation

Much to my chagrin, I found myself surrounded by professional dancers. The teacher demonstrated a series of steps. The

music began and the entire class moved as one, flying effort-
lessly through the combination. I was struck dumb and lifeless.
I wasn't sure I had seen all the steps, much less had time to
assimilate them. I made a valiant effort to do some kind of
movement to the music. Unfortunately, this was not one of
those "something is better than nothing" situations. I prayed to
God for a miracle: I asked that the floor open and I be
devoured. I remember one male dancer who made it a point to
stand next to me and sigh heavily. I got the message. I didn't
belong. No one had ever taught me the basics.

When I called my friend to ask why she had told me to
take this particular class, she said she thought it would be good
for me. "When professional dancers come back to New York
from road tours, they always review the basics in these classes."
She said constant reviewing kept them from getting sloppy and
falling into bad habits. Obviously, the cart had been put in
front of the horse.

What does this have to do with organizing an office?
Everything.

Mastering the Basics

It is the rare client who does not express embarrassment
within the first 15 minutes of our time together. I will
inevitably hear some variation on this theme: "Have you *ever*
seen anything like *this* before?" The answer is "All the time!" It
is often difficult to convince my clients. Our society has labeled
those who are not well organized as people who should be
ashamed of themselves. If you accept this, you may as well
believe that skills are learned by osmosis and practice is a waste
of time, that world-class athletes don't need to spend long
hours honing their skills, and that musicians don't need to
practice their instruments. Absurd, isn't it?

Entire books have been published on the setup and maintenance of a perfectly run office. We are limited in scope here
to the length of one chapter. In our examination of *time*, we
must establish realistic goals. I would hazard a guess that most
of these goals relate to the work aspect of your life. I believe a
solid technique must underlie everything you do to implement
these goals. I also want you to consider the physical space as
one of the keys to your success. *The work environment you
establish is a physical reflection of your desire to succeed. The best
file setup in the universe won't assist you if the room the files
reside in is a flash point of chaos.*

Every reader of this book finds him- or herself in a
unique work situation. Many of you toil in large corporations
with every electronic gadget at your disposal. Some of you are
lucky enough to have a secretary. At the other end of the spectrum, you might be someone like my dad after he retired. His
business life consisted of paying the bills and monitoring his
investments. *No matter how exalted or humble your business
environment, the basic principles used to lay a strong, organized
foundation are the same.* And practice does make perfect!

I would identify these principles as follows:

- Learn how to *eliminate* everything you do not need.
- Keep all material in related *categories* for ease in re-
  trieval.
- Develop *simple systems* to organize the categories.

Look familiar? It's the *magic formula* making its appearance in
the office. It is part of every chapter. Let's begin here with a
look at files.

Debris vs. Gold

A wonderful client admitted to me that he had tried to save money by researching the available books on organizing before he called me. "You know, Regina," he said, "these books drove me crazy. All of the authors seemed preoccupied with improving the condition of my files. My need was more basic. I wanted to know what a file was supposed to be!" My client isn't an idiot. He's a well-educated professional. If he didn't know what a file was, I realized it was a common concern. His honesty opened my eyes to the fact that this lack of basic (there's that word again) understanding was probably the root cause of the debris most of my clients face in their existing files.

Not long after this job was completed, I was hired to help an amazing woman organize her office. She was shifting from a private medical practice to the founding of a nonprofit organization. As we went through her files, I suggested the elimination of unneeded materials. She said to me, "When I was in medical school, there was a formula you followed to graduate. In life, no one ever showed me the formula for setting up an office." She was amazed by the fact that it was okay to toss old files. These two encounters helped shape this chapter.

Let me pose a series of questions.

What Is a File?

A file is a collection of related pieces of information. They should always be kept in alphabetical order. You want to keep any file you create lean and mean, full of the most up-to-date information. To help you retrieve this information on demand, related files should be grouped together.

What Do You Mean by Related Files?

Let me explain by sharing examples from the files of two of my clients. Harry manages a real estate office in an elegant beachside community outside Los Angeles. His office is very involved with the community. When we organized his files, I noticed that each community organization they worked with had a folder. These were stored alphabetically in the file cabinet with all the general information folders for the office. This is a good plan; however, it means opening several drawers of the cabinet should Harry wish to work with more than one of the organizations at a time. I made a label for a two-inch-wide box bottom hanging file folder called "Community Outreach" and placed all the community organizations there in alphabetical order. All related materials were now conveniently located in one place.

Jan is a medical consultant who had voluminous files to support her work. Here, too, everything was stored in alphabetical order. Jan, like Harry, had not noticed there were related pockets of information. For example, she has files for medical policies in several different states. If she wanted to compare the policies in California, New York, and Wisconsin on any given afternoon, the secretary would have to heave open three separate, long, heavy file drawers to access the information. I made a label called "Health Care, Individual States" and all of the information now lives in one box bottom hanging file folder.

What Is a Box Bottom Hanging Folder?

A hanging file folder is the dark green holder for the manila folders you use in file cabinets. It hangs on the long metal rods at each side. However, box bottom hanging file folders come in various widths at the bottom and can hold several related files comfortably. The bottom has a place for you to insert a piece of cardboard that keeps the surface flat to hold the folders. I suggest the two-inch version for the average office as a supplement to the regular hanging file folder. There are wider versions, but these generally work well in law or medical offices where the files are voluminous.

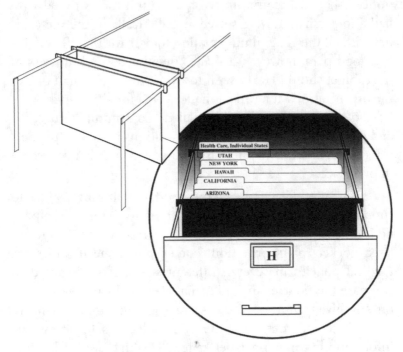

Box bottom hanging folder. (Please note: Box bottom hanging file folders do not work without the cardboard insert.)

Should I Use Box Bottom Exclusively?

In a word, no! You want to *supplement* with these only if you have materials that can reside in one compact area and therefore be easier for you to access. Sometimes I have two box bottoms lined up; other times I may have one box bottom followed by a single hanging file folder. The amount of information will dictate the size and number of the hanging file folders you need. The label alerts you to a change in subject. In other words, I could have had three full box bottom hanging file folders jammed with information about 26 of the 50 states in Jan's office. The first hanging file folder of any size that housed new information would have a new tab. Your eye scans these labels for the change in topics.

Printed labels are the easiest to read and give a tidy, calm appearance. You can purchase a label maker or generate them on your computer.

What About the Tabs You Mentioned?

Every box of hanging file folders will have a small bag of plastic tabs to use as a label. These are too short for my taste. I recommend you purchase a separate bag of the extra-long tabs. This will give you more freedom in creatively naming your files.

What Other Tools Can I Use to Help Identify My Files?

Color-coding files can be enormously helpful. Let's look at a few examples to see how this can be of assistance.

In his real estate office, Harry has an open door policy. In his private office, there is a four-drawer file cabinet. The first three drawers house material that might be of interest to the staff. They can enter at any time and look for information. They are also free to take files with them. The last drawer is where the personnel files are stored. These are for Harry's eyes and the office manager's eyes only. In Harry's desk are two file drawers filled with information he has created for his own reference. If Harry reentered his office and someone was leaving with a folder, there was no way for him to know without asking what file the agent had in his hands. I suggested we use colors to visually clue him in. Here's what it looked like:

- Manila folders were used for all general office information files.
- Green folders were enlisted to identify all personnel files.
- Red folders were used in Harry's desk to indicate high-priority information he had gathered and files of a restricted or personal nature.
- Blue folders indicated materials in Harry's desk that were for his eyes only. This information was not as immediate as the info in the red nor was it as sensitive in nature.

I made a list on Harry's hard drive of every file in his office. Here's how the file list is used:

- Harry maintains the list by adding the name of every new file and deleting any file that is tossed.
- He keeps an updated hard copy on his desk. It resides in a binder marked Reference. All key pieces of reference material are kept here. I like to prolong the life of these papers, not to mention their appearance, by slipping them into sheet protectors that are designed to fit in a binder.
- The hard copy of his files enables Harry to see the entire contents without getting up. When he wants to earmark things for his assistant to file, he knows exactly what label to put on the Post-it he will attach.
- If he wonders whether material has already been put in a folder, Harry has only to search his list.

It takes a bit of work to set this up, but it saves you time in the long run and definitely puts you in the power seat.

My files are color-coded as follows:

- Blue designates all of my organizing information.
- Green indicates my writing career.
- Manila houses my everyday business files.
- Yellow represents my acting career.

If I am looking for something in a hurry, I can ignore any color files that indicate information I am not concerned with at that moment. I frequently have an assistant work with me in the field, but rarely have anyone in my office. When I incorporate an assistant into my daily business life, he or she will be able to differentiate the various aspects of my work life at a glance.

How Do I Approach Each Paper?

Let's say you have a pile of papers on your desk. *One piece of paper at a time is the only way through a pile.* If you have 25 stacks, you can still only successfully deal with one piece of paper at a time, tackling one individual stack at a time.

How Do I Know What to Do with the Papers ... Even One at a Time?

You need to be realistic and ask yourself if you *really* need or want this piece of paper. If the inner prompt is to hold onto it, you need to understand why. For example, if it's a receipt for your taxes, the fact that you need to keep it is obvious. No extensive mental gymnastics need be applied. If it's a travel article to some exotic foreign city you long to go to, the answer may be slower coming.

Here are some common categories of files:

❧ Some of the papers you will come across as you sift through your piles will fall into the general category of action-provoking materials and these I place in my **action files.**

A general list of such files would include the following:

1. Calls
2. To Do: Immediately
3. To Do: Next Week
4. To Do: Low Priority
5. File
6. Reading
7. Bills

You may have other categories or you may want to eliminate one or two from my list. Some of my clients like to have these files in red folders to indicate their importance. I keep these files in my desk. I like to stay in my office and work rather than go into another room. If, like me, you work at home, you might like to have the freedom to wander with your action files. At the office supply store, you'll find small, portable file containers that can sit on top of the desk or be carried to the garden to make phone calls. Be sure you purchase one with closed sides. You don't want to leave a trail of papers as you walk from home to garden.

❧ Depending on your personal financial setup, your tax consultant or CPA will have a specified amount of time for you to hold onto your **tax receipts.** I keep the actual returns in a fireproof box in my office. The backup receipts are stored in a separate, heavy-duty plastic storage box. When the current tax year is filed, I place the backup receipts in this box, the oldest receipts are tossed, and my copy of the return goes into the metal box. Your tax person will be able to guide you in selecting the expenses that are legitimate tax deductions. I keep mine in separate envelopes marked for each category. All of the envelopes are tucked into a box bottom hanging file folder in the drawer of my desk where I keep my action files. The latter are in a box bottom hanging file folder in the front of the drawer. Behind them, in alphabetical order, are all the everyday files and/or critical papers I want to have at my fingertips.

- **Travel articles** are saved by just about everyone in a box or in one voluminous file. I divided my own articles several years ago into areas of the world:
  - Europe
  - Far East
  - USA
  - I created separate files for articles about Los Angeles and New York City. I access both frequently. Leafing through a voluminous file for the entire USA would be a time-wasting task. A smaller file also eliminates the chance I'll miss something.

In general, I have fewer articles in all categories than I used to because now I can cruise the Internet for the latest information. Restaurants close and museum hours change, so be astute when you cut out your articles.

- **Recipes** seem to collect in every home. You can file them in categories like these:

    * Main course

    * Salads

    * Sauces and dressings

    * Hors d'oeuvres

    * Desserts and so on

Should you wish to experiment, you don't have to thumb through hundreds of *neatly cutout* recipes. I'd ask the cooks to remember that the Internet is a great source for recipes as well. I'd also ask you to look at the number of cookbooks you now own. Ask yourself the last time you used a recipe you cut out of a magazine. The answers are as individual as the cooks asking them!

What Procedure Do I Follow for Setting Up New Files?

If you are just starting out or are creating a new project, brainstorm on paper before you start making labels. Again, look over your list and see how you can combine information. In the household management section of your files, you can pool information. For example, keep all family medical files together, gather all types of insurance information into one group (autos, boat, house, jewelry, and so on), or create a section for your warranties. As this can become a rather large, confusing file, separate your warranties/owner's manuals out by type:

    * TV/VCR

    * Office equipment

    * Computer

    * Stereo equipment

- Household purchases
- Appliances

You can add or delete categories according to the individual needs of your living situation and the number of people in your household.

How Can I Improve the Files I Have Now?

The best way to get control over your files is to clean them out one by one. I'm sure a number of files contain material you can now discard. Please consider the creation of archival files for material you'd like to hold on to but won't be accessing on a regular basis. As you return the files you intend to keep, write out an exact list of your existing files. When the list is complete, you can study it to see where you might create what I call master categories like Harry's Community Outreach file. Don't forget to create the handy hard copy for reference.

Can You Elaborate on the Concept of Archival Files?

Be sure you aren't saving too many outdated papers. Remember what we said about your old clothes? If you aren't a famous movie star, the value is probably nil. Business files are sometimes kept as a kind of memorabilia. Be realistic about the personal value. Consider the expenditure of time as well as emotional and physical energy you are demanding of those who will one day be sorting out these treasures.

Once you have your archival materials set aside, you'll need a place to store everything. I recommend the new plastic storage units if you don't have a spare file cabinet for this express purpose. Boxes will be destroyed over time. You'll be saving yourself the task of transferring these files to another box in the future if you purchase the plastic containers. (As an aside, let me add that the same principal holds true for holiday ornament storage. They can be stored practically forever in these new plastic containers. My personal favorites are the ones with wheels. They come in small, medium, and large.)

How Often Do I Need to Clean Out Existing Files?

A cathartic purge should be done on a regular basis. I have heard of someone who organizes his 95-year-old mother's files every 6 months when he goes to visit. This is a tad zealous for my taste.

Even if you work for a large, busy corporation or the CIA, where I imagine there are voluminous files growing on a daily basis, I would suggest a yearly purge. It's a very individual issue based on the volume and speed of incoming materials. For the average person with personal, home, and business-related files, I'd suggest somewhere between one and two years maximum.

Lessons from the Garden

Many of my clients balk at the news that they will have to periodically purge their files. This is especially true for first-timers. They find the process of setting up files so arduous, they can't imagine electing to face it again. Here's one of my favorite analogies. I love to garden. I can spend an entire day weeding, pruning, re-potting, sweeping, and so on. I survey my work and feel a sense of accomplishment and joy. I maintain my plants with great care. Every few weeks, however, it is as if they have grown wild overnight and I must once again devote time to their care. **Don't think of your files as inert paper matter. Think of them as vital, energetic stores of information.** You want to keep them current, clean, and state-of-the-art organized.

What About the Placement of the File Cabinet?

Let me tell you the story of Dolores. She hated her home office and yet needed to spend considerable time there. Dolores works outside the home in the technical end of the movie industry. Her home office is where she must keep the research materials she uses in her work. It is here she works to secure the next film she'll be working on. In addition, she has outside business interests and needs to track the information with well-maintained files.

Physically, her office had an interesting twist. The desk was situated next to a built-in book case. Opening the left-side drawers meant a struggle because they would always bump into the end of the bookcase. This was a small office with every bit of space utilized. We needed those drawers to function. We had nowhere else to put the desk. What to do?

I noticed that the folders she had placed in the left-side file drawer were the ones she needed to access on a daily basis. The files in the right side of her desk rarely needed. I pointed out that if she switched these files, the problem would be solved. You see, the right side currently had two separate categories of files that were not destined to grow very much. The left-side drawer would open far enough for her to access this material whenever she needed it. Since that wouldn't be very often, the irritation factor was reduced.

You should also consider whether you are left- or right-handed and place the most frequently used items at your fingertips. Why have your phone on the right side of the desk if you're a lefty like me? You'll be unconsciously irritated every time you have to reach across the desk.

What Else Constitutes the Basic Furniture Setup for a Home Office?

- You'll certainly need a good size desk and a comfortable chair. I like a chair that rolls and the plastic sheets that fit under the desk. Whenever possible, I want my clients to have immediate access to all the files and equipment in their office. If you can eliminate 10 trips a day across the room to a file cabinet that could be within rolling distance at your side, why not save this time?

- It creates a good impression to have separate phone lines for your home and your business.

- Depending on the size of your business, the file drawer in your desk might be adequate to house information. My retired father would have been quite happy with this much space. As noted, I keep my action files next to me. In addition, I have a couple of small, two-drawer file cabinets in my office. All organizing and writing materials are stored in one. The other cabinet is for personal business and miscellaneous information.

- Have you noticed a high volume of trips to the local copy store? You might need to purchase a copier.

- Visual people often utilize a bulletin board as a place for images that inspire.

- We'll be able to adapt some of the practices we employ here to make the bathroom and kitchen work efficiently. Remember the following steps when you read the later chapters. After all, all knowledge is one, right?

  1. Don't forget to line the drawers of your desk to avoid the slip 'n' slide drama.

  2. Keep basic office supplies at hand, but establish a supply storage area nearby to hold the bulk of your purchases.

3. Toss excess packaging.

4. Use containers in your desk and/or in the supply closet. They will assist in your efforts to establish organized categories.

5. Have a nice big trash can.

This list is just a primer. If your sole business activity is opening the mail and paying the bills, most of the previous information is simply clutter for you. If you are running a business out of your home other than a consulting one like mine, you may need all of the this section's material. Needless to say, in corporate America the list of necessary gizmos grows every day.

Bogey Man in the Office

I have friends and clients who refuse to touch a computer. For those readers who are computer-phobic, I urge you to investigate the reasonably priced classes at your local community college. If you pride yourself on being able to teach yourself, there are a number of "how-to" books published on the subject. Using a PC or Mac, you will have the opportunity to explore the Internet and get e-mail. You can even fax from your computer. This will save you the purchase of a separate piece of equipment. If your business needs to store more information and your space is limited, you can always have the data scanned onto discs for later access in the computer. Many magazines and periodicals are now available on disc or via the Internet. There are lots of creative ways a computer can help you save time and money. It's also more fun than I can describe in words. Why do you think some of us get lost for hours? You don't have to be a genius to reap tremendous benefits from this marvelous machine. A computer opens up your communication abilities like nothing else can. This can be a pretty scary topic for some folks. I imagine some of you are sweating the way I did in that dance class. Let's take a mini-break together and I'll tell you a story.

My Lebanese Grandmother

Jenny Sawaya spoke five languages fluently. She had an absolutely fearless nature when it came to creating a better life for herself. She traveled to South America to live with older siblings who had previously emigrated to Brazil. Not finding the life she wanted, she returned to Lebanon. In a few years, she set sail once again. This time the destination was America. She made these long voyages alone, traveling in steerage. Jenny was still a teenager the day she landed in New York to start her new life.

My grandmother told me countless stories about her travels. I think she gave me her wanderlust. Something about her, however, always puzzled me. The same woman who was a fearless world traveler had been afraid to learn to read and write. She could not read the newspaper, check her children's homework, or even write a letter home. She spoke five languages like a native and could not read or write a word in any of them.

In the next millennium, a lack of fundamental computer skills will leave you out of the loop. Don't be like my Lebanese grandmother. Embrace all the challenges life sets before you.

Now let's return and take a minute to examine some home and corporate offices I have organized. See if your situation resembles any I describe here.

Uncle Sam and the Lacy Lingerie

Several years ago, a school principal called me with an interesting problem. She said her school office was organized and ran efficiently. Allison also maintained an office at home. For some reason, she found it impossible to work there. This was of enormous significance as she wished to write a book and plan a series of teaching seminars. I said I would stop by and see if I could identify the problem.

I follow my instincts in new surroundings. I wanted to tour the downstairs part of the house before seeing the home office that was located on the second floor. Allison's bedroom was extremely feminine and inviting. I could easily imagine her resting in this room after a hard day's work with a good book or a fashion magazine. When we opened her top dresser drawer, however, I almost had cardiac arrest. There, nestled amid her beautiful lingerie, were income tax receipts! I could only imagine the assault on her senses first thing in the morning as she reached in for the day's underwear and had to wade through business receipts. Allison explained this was more evidence of her not wanting to be in her home office. Now my curiosity had been peaked. I could hardly wait to see this infamous room.

The door opened and the problem was immediately evident. In the center of a modest-size room was a queen-size bed. To the left of the entry, in the near corner, was a tiny desk good for displaying antiques or family photos but useless as a place to accomplish anything. The far-right wall was a closet with sliding glass, mirrored doors. I knew without looking it was filled with "stuff." Scattered around, in every available space, was exercise equipment.

Identity Crisis

It was not a mystery to me why Allison did not like being there nor why she was not productive when she did force herself to spend time there. This room had no designated purpose and its energy was confused. If the room is set up to be confusing, the work done there will be poor in quality. This is the most common mistake I see in the setup of a home office.

The Setup

The home office can be used as a adjunct to the main working space, which is elsewhere, or it can be the principal place of conducting business. In either case, I believe it should be carefully planned rather than adding the function of work to a room already burdened by other demands. For example, it was extremely thoughtful of Allison to keep a queen-size bed for her mother's annual visit. For the two weeks Mom was in residence, she would feel most welcome and no doubt sleep like a baby. This gift, however, meant that 50 weeks out of the year, Allison would not be able to use her home office. Realistically, with that huge bed, there was barely room to turn around, much less to think creatively. Your working area reflects your mental attitude about what you hope to accomplish.

Allison was giving lip service to a writing career. Her lack of commitment was evident to me the minute I opened the door. Just before I began to work on *The Zen of Organizing*, I developed pneumonia. Anyone who has ever had this illness can tell you that it takes several weeks to regain your strength. Staying perfectly organized was not my highest priority in the first weeks as I could barely stay awake. When I was ready to start a daily commitment to writing, I had to restore order to my files and papers. Not only can I not think in the midst of chaos, I would be a complete hypocrite if I tried to teach others the art of order while struggling in a sea of confusion. It is no different for you. Whether you are writing a book or selling Mary Kay cosmetics, **your environment must be set up to help you achieve your goal. If you give your goal the honor and respect it deserves, it will be easier to achieve.**

I gave Allison several suggestions to improve the working conditions of this room:

- I felt a high-quality futon sofa might serve her purposes here. She could get up periodically and sit there to do paperwork and brainstorm her book. The futon would also be her mother's bed when she came to visit.

- The closet had to be cleaned out. Half the contents were donated to a charity. The other half stayed, but were shifted to the far side where the contents were organized should they ever be needed again. Allison and her spouse had purchased camping and skiing equipment over the years, abandoning each endeavor after a few experiences. I would have preferred to see the equipment go to the garage. The near side became the supply closet. (You can easily create shelf space in a closet for the storage of supplies. Lay wooden boards across wall braces, or place a small bookcase inside the closet.)

- Allison's home had no other place for the exercise equipment, so we arranged all of it in one part of the room. The visual trick here is that the office furniture occupied the left as you entered and the workout area was to your right. There are all sorts of ways to make categories.

- I felt she needed a better desk and a more comfortable chair. Writing is hard work and if you are physically uncomfortable while you do it, you are stacking the deck against your stated goal. I can't imagine being successful at any serious endeavor if I am physically uncomfortable.

If a client resists all suggestions for improvement, I know it is time to back off the issue. One of two dynamics is at play: Most likely, they have no real desire to accomplish the stated goals. The other possibility is they were taught as children that it is only through suffering that anything worthwhile is accomplished. Time will tell the tale.

Home Away from Home

If you are like most people in an office situation, you have an in-and-out box with unknown treasures stuffed inside the bottom tray and a pile reaching to the sky in the top one. Let me offer some help. Piles erupt for three reasons:

- ❧ You have never set up the files that should house this information.
- ❧ You have the files and are either too busy or too lazy to put things away.
- ❧ You do not understand the purpose of an in-and-out box.

You have been armed with the information necessary to help you establish good, working files. You need to set aside the time to create the system. Once it is in place, instead of casually tossing papers in these trays, you can earmark them for the appropriate destination. Is it a bill to be paid? Is it something you need to do? Is it reading matter? Does it get filed? Now you see that the work indicated previously was leading you to this place of control in all areas of your office involving the paper puzzle.

What Is the Purpose of the In-and-Out Box?

The in-and-out box is meant to be a "physical conversation" with another human being. In one part of the box, you place all the information you want your secretary or assistant to be aware of that has crossed your path. As you deal with these papers, you make notations on Post-its as to the appropriate destination. Working with the hard copy of your files nearby, you'll be very precise in your directives. Papers that get stacked will inevitably dissolve into chaotic piles. Be sure therefore that you are indeed communicating with each other and keeping both sections of the in-and-out box cleaned out.

Your secretary or assistant will have the other part of the in-and-out box to leave papers that you need. In large corporations, the mail will be opened and notations made for the boss. If the in-and-out tray is too small for the amount of mail, there are other creative ways of dealing with the delivery of the mail. Here's one that works well for some people, especially in a small or home-based office.

Size Matters

Got your attention, didn't I? In some situations, I suggest a decent-size basket as a repository for the morning mail. Once I purchased a basket for a couple who had a home office. He works at the studios and she is a full-time mom. From this home office, they ran their personal business affairs. As I was organizing the entire house, I would check in each week with areas I had completed. From time to time, a solution needs to be tweaked a bit to better support the personalities involved. I almost fell over when I saw my basket had been replaced with one three times its size. I had said that it was okay for mail to pile up here for a few days if a family or work emergency arose. The mail would be in one contained area and easier to get caught up with when normal scheduling resumed. Our deal had included one caveat: When there was no longer any room in the basket, it was time to deal with its contents. Obviously, if you have a wicker bath tub on your desk, it will be weeks before you are forced to deal with incoming mail. Be prudent. Learn to consider the beauty of medium size.

Bill Paying

Dealing with money is an issue for many of my clients. One of the most interesting clients I had was a composer who had no interest in organizing his papers. His wife was extremely organized and had trouble understanding his lack of concern as papers piled up on his desk. I was asked to see what I could do to get his desk tidy and functioning.

The mystery to me was the fact that he was not only a composer, but an arranger. In both arenas you must have an extremely well-organized view of what you want to accomplish. You must also stay on top of myriad details. This lovely man taught me something I have learned to apply to every client in a similar situation.

The simple truth is that some people are so detail-oriented in the work area of their lives that continuing that order in their home life is mentally overwhelming. They need a place to relax. George said the organization of his desk was of no interest to him nor would he be inclined to maintain the order if it were established for him. Looking at the contents of his desk revealed two things: Here he dealt with his hobbies and paid his bills. Actually, he paid his bills when he could find them or when he happened to remember they were due! George made more than enough to pay his life expenses. He was concerned that his credit rating would suffer if bills were not paid simply because he forgot. We turned his bill paying over to a CPA firm. Now George has only to check a monthly statement to be sure the amounts paid are in line with his expectations. The CPA firm also has automatic access to his tax-deductible expenses. The preparation of his income tax therefore becomes less labor-intensive for him.

This arrangement would not be a comfortable one for every client. No matter the individual solution you choose for paying your bills, the bottom line is to be consistent. Some of my clients pay everything due on the first of the month; others divide bill paying between the first and the fifteenth of each month. This solution means all of your incoming bills can be placed in one file as they arrive.

I like a slightly more complicated approach. You aren't surprised, are you? I make a note in a separate calendar when each bill must be paid so that it will arrive by its due date. Every evening I check this calendar to see what needs to be sent out the next day. This is a good solution for the control freak in the crowd. Don't forget to trash all the extraneous materials that arrive with your bills. You do not need the envelope it arrived in or the advertisements that were stuffed inside (including the one attached to the return envelope). If the payment is a tax deduction, the statement can be filed. Lean and mean works well outside the gym as well.

Instant Communication

The ease with which we communicate now is absolutely breathtaking. I remain astounded that a document I create on my computer can be sent around the world in seconds. Like all gifts, however, there can be a downside, and instant communication poses a few. Our e-mail, voice mail, fax communications, and daily calls can drown us if we lose control. Let's take a brief look at the dynamics involved.

You need to establish a game plan for your day. Each day well lived moves you closer to your goal. Like a skilled emergency room physician, your work environment must be set up to help you achieve success. Whatever you need is at hand. What you need to accomplish has been charted. When the ER doctor arrives for his shift, he is told who is in the area and decides what order he needs to see his patients. My migraine can wait while your broken leg is set. No matter how carefully he establishes his schedule with the staff, if a car crash victim or a gunshot wound bursts through the doors, the plan must instantly be adjusted. It would not be remotely appropriate for a doctor to say he could not save the life of the person with the gunshot wound because he had Regina's migraine next on his to-do list.

Your daily work life is no different. Every communication can be empowered by you to completely disrupt your day. If you have done the work of establishing true goals, your daily work life will have direction. Ask yourself the following questions:

- Will responding to this phone call, e-mail, and so on take me away from my ultimate goals or move me closer?

- Are all of these interruptions really emergencies or am I avoiding my work load?

- Am I completely unable to say no to another's requests?

Establish daily time segments devoted to returning phone calls, reading fax transmissions, and responding to e-mail. These routines should be interrupted for true emergencies only.

The Boss Who Could and the Secretary Who Refused

Binnie works in one of corporate America's cubicles. When we met, I was deeply concerned about the amount of work I perceived she was being asked to perform. Her desk was piled with papers. Her files were jammed with information. Her work area, including under the counter, was filled with stacked boxes and personal possessions. It is not possible to think clearly in this type of environment. Visual chaos makes it difficult to function.

No matter what approach I used, Binnie was entrenched. She could not part with paper. She would not move things to other locations. When I secured permission for my computer consultant to come in and do her data entry for her, she never made time in her schedule. I began to realize that Binnie liked her situation. Walking by her cubicle, anyone would feel sorry for her. She stayed late into the evening to try and catch up. She said there wasn't enough time during the day to keep up with her workload. Spending time with her, I realized Binnie had no direction in her day. She had no idea what the appropriate amount of time might be to allocate to a task. Miscellaneous phone calls would last for 30 minutes. Factor two or three of those calls into a day and you see why she stayed until midnight to try and catch up. Stacks of papers and jammed files were her badges of hard work. She had no intention of parting with her situation. In her mind, she would demonstrate a change after she successfully manipulated the situation and was ensconced in her own office. I had to abandon my efforts to help her. You cannot impose order on a mind attached to chaos and drama.

Are you like Binnie? Are you married to the physical drama of a chaotic work life? Do you identify yourself with the struggle that flows naturally out of this chaos? There are some things no book on organizing, no matter how well intentioned, can heal. You decide to change. You make a commitment to the process that will allow this change to occur.

Binnie warned me that her boss would not part with a single piece of paper. I was terrified. Much to my surprise and delight, what transpired was a completely different scenario. Steve had been overwhelmed by sudden changes in his personal life. Dealing with these situations had caused a temporary inability to function full-tilt at work. Piles of papers were everywhere in his office. They had even begun inhabiting boxes that were threatening to overrun the office. Steve made a commitment to work with me. We examined one piece of paper at a time. It was a joyous process to watch this man restore his work environment to order. Frequently, getting organized is so overwhelming that my clients need me for direction and as a kind of cheerleader. I'm the guide who leads you out of the chaotic woods into the simplicity of the clearing.

Steve's office was restored in short order. He has maintained the systems we put in place. He understands, too, that Binnie will change when she makes a commitment to herself. Until then, all the organizing consultants in the world cannot help her.

Creativity Compromised

There are clients who are resistant to change based on false concepts. My personal favorite is the artist who swears to me that becoming organized will force a loss of creativity. Even his friends assure me that "So-and-so is an artist. You know *they* can't be organized!" As an organized artist, I can assure you from personal experience that **being in an orderly mental and physical environment frees the soul to seek the highest level of creativity possible.** I am not so arrogant that I judge this on my personal experience alone. I would ask the artists in chaos to look at the lives of the most successful designers on Seventh Avenue. Here we find men and women who turn the fashion industry on its ear while running multimillion-dollar business enterprises. Look, too, at the artists in the film industry who act, produce, write, and direct their own films. At the highest levels of accomplishment in any artistic endeavor, you will find people who have integrated their creative and their business sides. They are goal oriented, delegate appropriately, and know they cannot do it all alone. These are my mentors. We must each choose those whose life experience we wish to emulate.

Final Note

My goal with this chapter has been to present you with the tools you'll need to design a space and create work habits that will support rather than sabotage your career. May you feel tremendous love for whatever you believe you have been called here to do.

和平

Peace

CHAPTER 4

Closets

*"Many things
which cannot be overcome
when they are together,
yield themselves up
when taken little by little."*

—*Plutarch*

When my mother allowed me to invade her closet and play dress up with her beautiful clothes, I was in seventh heaven. I loved my mother's clothes. She always looked sophisticated and fashionable. Seeing her at a distance made me smile. "That's *my* mom," I thought, chest swelling with pride.

Dress Up

Even now, I can close my eyes and recall that everything smelled like Chanel #5, the fragrance my mother wore every day. I remember the predominance of autumn colors like dark brown, hunter green, gold, and holiday red. My mother always said that inanimate objects would have interesting tales to tell if they could speak. It seemed to me that each article of clothing in her closet did indeed have a story to tell. None would have been more touching than the tale her fur coat might have told.

On cold winter mornings, the street outside my grammar school was closed to traffic. All eight grades would play under the watchful eyes of the nuns. I didn't know how to join in, so I'd stand in front of my mom and lean against her for protection. My mother would wrap her fur coat around me and from the shelter of this sweet coat, I observed the world. As you can see, I had a relationship with clothing from an early age.

I also had a relationship with my mother's closet. As I mentioned earlier in the Introduction, it amazed me that my neat mother had an ongoing tornado in her closet. You never saw a pile of anything in our home, but you needed a road map to find an article of clothing. Over the years I have discovered that a closet is more than just an area in the home where clothes are stored. It is in many ways an accurate picture of the person's inner life. My mother's home would lead you to believe she was Martha Stewart incarnate. Her closet told you that her private world was in turmoil.

Life Stories Revealed

Organizing a closet for a new client is like reading a great mystery novel. No matter how much I think I have figured out who this human being before me is, I will more often than not be surprised. I will discover the blueprint of their lives hidden in their closets. Let me tell you the story of the actress with the dark clothes.

This lady is known for the excellence of her work. She is talented, respected, and capable in dramatic roles as well as comedic ones. In person, there is something "light" about her being. She is fun to be with and deeply caring. When I organize a closet, the way through that overwhelming "whole" is to take one item at a time and decide its fate. As we cleaned out Anita's closet, I noticed something astonishing. Everything she was discarding was dark in color and the fabrics were heavy. They reminded me of the clothes I might have worn back home in New York in the late fall. They felt out of place in sunny, warm Los Angeles. After an hour or so, I asked if she had purchased all of these clothes at the same time. She told me the following story.

"When I married my husband, I assumed it was forever. One day he came home and announced that he wanted a divorce. I was completely taken by surprise. For the next three years, I tried to recover from the shock and rebuild my life. It was during this time that I purchased all these clothes." I told her she was long past her period of mourning. It was time to purchase clothes that reflected who she truly was. The next time I saw her, her newly organized closet had been filled with light-colored clothes in airy fabrics that let the world know visually who she was before a word of introduction could be uttered.

Every closet tells a story. I'll share another anecdote to help you understand more clearly. I had a client in her early 60s who was a true clothes pack rat. She had a lovely figure, but middle age had seen the disappearance of her waist. In a drawer, however, neatly packed away were all of the cashmere sweaters she had worn in high school. I pointed out that most of them had moth holes. I felt this was a more elegant reason to suggest throwing them away than pointing out that she would never fit into them again in this lifetime. She said she could not part with them. I countered with the idea perhaps she could hold on to one of them. The others could be tossed. "Oh, no," she said, "I'll have them repaired!" After several days of this kind of discovery and discussion (she had lots of closets!), I realized that she was holding on to the past. Articles of clothing represented times in her life now gone forever. If she still had a specific garment, in her mind she held a piece of that experience captive in her hands. One who is this attached to the past is not fully present in the current moment; and this moment is all we truly ever have.

When people ask me what the "rules" are for tossing unworn clothes, I tell them everyone is unique and I have no rules. As you can see from the stories I shared, what we have in our closets and drawers must be sifted through patiently and gently until the need to toss or restore is revealed. If you don't enjoy this sort of detective work, you might want to hire some-one like me to help you make decisions and keep the process moving. I have one more story to share and then I'll give you my list of tips for the creation of a perfect closet.

I had a friend for many years who crammed clothing into closets and drawers like no one else I have ever known. Watching her literally fight her way through a crunch of clothes was a feat to behold. Long before I ever dreamed I'd become a professional organizer, I begged her to let me put her things in order. Her closet was actually worse than my mother's! It was as if a storm of great magnitude had blown through the area. My offers always fell on deaf ears. She liked the struggle. I think it made her feel unique.

The minute you wake up in the morning, the possibility exists that things beyond your control may go wrong. Some days they are major problems; other days it can be just the irri-tation of getting stuck in traffic. If I am having a bad morning, I am calmed the minute I enter my walk-in closet. No matter the chaos of the moment, I never add fuel to the flame by cre-ating the drama of the lost article of clothing. I want you to face all of the unexpected, uncontrollable chaos from a base of peace. *If you open your closet and are instantly confronted with a battlefield, you will unconsciously be churning the emotional waters.* A potentially bad day can escalate quickly into a com-plete disaster after a closet battle.

The Good Purge

Clean out your closets and drawers on a regular basis. Donate usable items to a charity where they will have a new life with someone less fortunate. You will have a tax deduction and more space for the new things wending their way to you. Put everything to be given away in heavy-duty trash bags and take them out of the house as soon as possible. When I first started, I was amazed to see how many items earmarked for charity magically migrated back to their original places of honor. Now I remove everything for the client and mail them the tax receipt.

Baby Clothes

Even women amazingly adept at parting with possessions will have problems with their children's baby clothes. I have never had children, but I can imagine the separation pangs this particular parting causes. I suggest to moms that they might want to box and store the clothes until they are ready to see them go to another child. If you are emotional about this issue, be comforted by the knowledge that it's difficult for just about everyone.

Size Wars

Women more than men tend to have several different sizes in their closets. They always ask me what I think they should do with their "skinny" clothes (no one saves the "fat" clothes). If you haven't been "skinny" in a long time, I would suggest you part with those clothes. After all, when you return to a more desirable weight, why would you want to wear outdated clothes? When was the last time you heard someone say, "I'm so proud of my new body, I think I'll drape it in my old clothes."

Fake Prosperity

Very often people unconsciously keep their closets jammed full of outdated and never-worn or rarely worn clothing because the sheer volume gives them a sense of security. "I must be prosperous," the unconscious mind shouts. "Look at all the stuff I have!" Learn to trust in yourself and in the universe. You are loved and provided for and it has nothing to do with the stuff jammed into your closets and drawers.

Let's pretend you have cleaned out your clothes. Let's see what we can do to make the closets and drawers inviting.

Checklist for a Beautiful Closet

☐ Use one-color, thick, plastic hangers.

☐ Avoid wire hangers.

☐ Remove the plastic covers the cleaners send home with your clothes; if your clothes need to be covered (such as summer whites), place them in canvas bags.

☐ Face all clothes in one direction.

☐ Group by type of clothing (skirts, jackets, vests, blouses, suits, and so on). Some women must keep outfits together; others are willing to separate skirts and jackets and create new combinations.

☐ Organize each group by color, starting with white and ending in black; use the same color progression in every area.

☐ Start with sleeveless, graduate to short sleeves, and end with long.

☐ Get shoes off the floor! Stacking racks are wonderful; canvas shoe bags that hang on the back of the closet door work well. If you have the space and are the type who needs to see an item to remember it exists, try clear-plastic shoe boxes.

Closet Design

Needless to say, every closet is different and without actually seeing yours, my comments must be general. I'm sure you'll find some tidbits here that will help you keep your clothes in order. Let's go over the following closet checklist:

☐ Is there an enormous space between the top shelf and the ceiling in the closet? Install another shelf and use it for everyday items or seasonal storage, depending on its height. This shelf can be a piece of plain lumber set on two wall braces.

☐ Do you have mirrored, sliding glass doors on your closet? Starting at the far right, set your clothes up with the things you'll grab first. Work back in the order of retrieval. This will prevent you from sliding the doors back and forth looking for one item stored at the far right, the next at the far left, the next on the right side in the middle, and so on. These closets are a pain and if your budget allows, have doors installed.

☐ With drawer space at a premium, most of my clients store sweats and sweaters in neat stacks on closet shelves. These neat stacks tend to fall apart the minute the first item is retrieved. To prevent this, go to a store that sells closet supplies and purchase some shelf dividers. They are about eight inches high and slip onto the shelf, creating an instant wall between the stacks of clothing. While you're at it, keep these stacks in color groups just as you did the clothes hanging in your closet. This is visually calming and makes retrieval very easy.

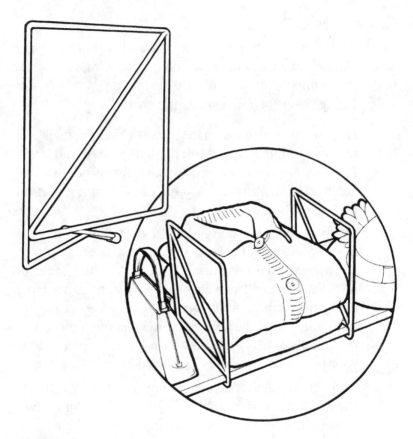

Shelf divider.

☐ Instead of stacking woolen sweaters unprotected, put them in clear-plastic containers. The colors will be visible and you can toss in some mothballs for protection.

☐ To avoid a jumble in drawers, there are wonderful items you can purchase that will keep things tidy. There are, for instance, plastic containers for bras, underwear, and socks. You can guess by now that I'm going to suggest you keep all items of the same color together. Women are often amazed at the number of white or black bras they actually do have. When the bras are in a jumble, it's hard to tell if you have 2 or 20.

☐ Items like belts and ties should be kept on hangers made for that purpose, or kept on units that can be installed, should you have the wall space. For women's belts that resist this type of solution, try a plastic container or even a wicker basket.

☐ If you've been blessed with a hall closet, keep your coats and jackets here. Grab whatever is appropriate for the day as you exit. This will free up an incredible amount of space in your clothes closet.

Closet solutions go on and on. Depending on your space, put hooks on your closet walls and hang seasonally appropriate hats. Some of my clients have closets that are bigger than studio apartments in New York City. I encourage anyone in that situation to put out a pretty vase on a shelf and add some silk flowers. Restore peace to your being every time you have to dress your body. After all, it is the vehicle for the soul.

The Clothing of the Dead

I was raised to give away the deceased's clothing immediately after the funeral unless a particular item held great value or special significance. I made an interesting exception for my father that taught me an important lesson. I like to think of this lesson as his last gift to me. My father realized he was dying before the doctors did. He told the neighbors he knew the end was near. They shared his words with me: "I know my diabetes has finally caught up with me." My strong father wept into tissues and then tucked them into the pockets of his winter coat.

I was so touched by this story when I heard it that I was unable to part with that coat or those precious tissues. Five years later, I decided to sell the house my parents had retired to when they left Brooklyn. My mother had passed away the year after my father died. As I prepared to move their household back to New York City, I looked at that coat differently. It was as if someone had thrown cold water over me. Was my father being honored by my saving used tissues? I tossed them at last and gave the coat to charity.

My father had given me many beautiful pieces of jewelry. I will always have some of the furniture he bought for our home. As a human being, I am his representative in the world: the physical marker he passed this way. I'm sure wherever he was, my father was relieved. Would you want your used tissues enshrined after your death? If you are faced with decisions about the clothing and possessions of someone close to you who has now passed away, ask yourself if your choices bring honor to their memory.

The Cello Caper

The past can be represented by any collection of items, not just clothing. One of my clients wanted her husband to part with the cello he had played in his high school band. This rather large, unwieldy instrument was moved from house to house over the course of his life. Now it resides in the closet in his home office. He said he'd never part with it even though he had a brand-new one in the house for those times he was moved to play.

With his wife's permission, I decided to try an experiment. I took the cello home. For two weeks, he opened and closed the closet door and never noticed this precious artifact was missing. His wife and I were astonished. Finally, we asked him about it. He had actually never once noticed it wasn't there. Once he was told, he wasn't happy it was gone. I said I'd be delighted to return it. I wanted him, however, to consider an alternative. I suggested the cello be donated to a high school in Los Angeles with a professional music department. This sweet old instrument would have a new life in the hands of a young musician. My client so loved the idea, he not only gave his cello, but he made a generous donation to the department. New instruments could now be purchased for the coming semester.

Final Note

In my youth, I was very attached to the idea of having lots of clothes. I dreamed of having so many I'd need the same kind of electronic retrieval system used by professional cleaners to retrieve items. God graciously gave me the opportunity to unpack lots of wealthy clients who did indeed have more clothes than your local department store. Guess what? You can only wear one outfit at a time. And unless you have the social life of a corporate honcho, there just isn't any point to burdening your personal environment with all that stuff.

No matter how much clothing or how many possessions you have, no matter how beautiful you set it all up in the space available, here's the bottom line: If you are carrying around things you'll never wear again or use in this lifetime, you are cluttering your present experience with the energy of the past. *It's that simple. Free your space, and you'll free yourself.*

康

Health

CHAPTER 5

Bathrooms

*"In returning and rest
you shall be saved:
in quietness and in trust
shall be your strength."*

—Isaiah 30:15

As every parent who has ever raised a girl knows, we need our quality bathroom time. Every summer when we'd visit my mom's family in the country, I finally had a decent bathroom to monopolize. "What is she doing in there?" reverberated throughout the house all summer long as frustrated adults waited for my exit.

Fantasy Time

My maternal aunts and uncles lived on a working farm in the Allegheny mountains outside Pittsburgh. The farmhouse was modest in size, but oh that bathroom! It was huge by Brooklyn standards. It had a shower, a tub, lots of cabinets, and a large mirror. My aunts filled their cabinets with every girlie item you could possibly imagine. Here, in one place, were hair sprays and gels, rollers of every size and shape, enough makeup to open a store, and tons of mysterious lotions and potions my mother did not own. What else did a budding actress need? It was paradise. I wore everyone's makeup. I did wild things to my hair. I played out scenes with imaginary companions. It was a blast. Everyone thought I was weird.

The one thing I noted about this bathroom was that its inner structure was as chaotic as my mother's closet. Could this be hereditary, I wondered? Every item seemed to have been tossed into the cupboards without any rhyme or reason. Inevitably, one of my aunts would drive to the store in a panic for some essential item, only to discover that there were indeed two or three packages hidden away in another cupboard across the room. Isn't there an easier way, I wondered?

The Temple of the Soul

Few people give much thought to the importance of creating order in the bathroom. Your body is the temple of the soul. Preparing it for presentation to the world is not an unimportant task. Fighting through mounds of makeup in a drawer or running out of soap or toilet paper can really set a day on its ear. We tend to think of a bathroom as the room where necessary functions are performed, not a place of tremendous emotional and spiritual significance.

Imagine, if you will, that you have run out of your favorite fragrance or after-shave. You drive to your local department store. An improbable sight greets you. The individual cosmetic displays look as if all the lotions and potions have been hurled onto the counters in a mad frenzy. Used makeup sponges, tissues, and Q-tips litter every available space. The garbage containers are overflowing. Unidentifiable sticky residues adorn the exact spot you rest your arm. You move and your sleeve is instantly coated with five new lipstick shades. It's a jarring experience. Would you be moved to sort through the fragrant rubble and search for treasures? Or would you be irritated at the sight and run screaming from the store?

I have one question for you: Why would you do this to yourself at home? Let's create a retreat where you can rest your
weary soul.

Lessons of the Quake

Two years after the Northridge earthquake rocked Los Angeles,
I received a call from a wonderful couple. June and Todd are
both high-level corporate executives who work uncon-
scionably long hours. The earthquake of January 17 had nearly
destroyed their home. The repairs needed had been so extensive that they were forced to move to a rental house. Now they
were ready to return home.

They did not wish to spend their evenings and weekends
trying to get organized. They realized, however, that in order to
keep up with their schedules, they needed to have an unclut-
tered environment. June and Todd had placed all of their
belongings in storage. As human beings, we have a vast array of
personal items we feel we just cannot live without. Not only
were June and Todd returning home with all of their original
possessions, they were adding two years of miscellaneous purchases to the household. I was hired to restore order.

I asked June if she would make a list of projects and
arrange them in order of importance. We agreed on absolutely
everything except one detail. Like most people, June saw the
bathroom as a room she passed through during the course of
a day. I see it as a key element in maintaining a sense of order
and peace in the house. After all, where do we head in the
morning, minutes after our eyes open? And where do we stop
en route to our beds at day's end? June understood my point of
view and allowed me to move the organization of the master
bath into the top five priorities.

Clearing the Way

Let's examine the steps you might follow to get your bathroom organized, no matter what the size or current condition. These are, by the way, the same guidelines I followed to organize June and Todd:

- Create a work station before you begin. Clear off the counter, bring in a table, or make a space available on the floor. Be creative. Be comfortable.

- Have a few heavy-duty trash bags handy.

- Wherever possible, remove the outer packaging from items you wish to store in the bathroom. You'll be surprised at the amount of unnecessary cardboard and plastic wrap you'll be tossing. For example, I recently purchased a bottle of self-tanning lotion at a department store. The bottle came in a large box with voluminous printed instructions. I read them as well as the version printed on the bottle's label. It was not necessary to clutter my bathroom with the insert or the box. In the same vein, sometimes two bottles of a product get shipped in one box. Take one bottle out to use and store the other. The huge box, if saved, would once again be an example of something you do not need that is taking up valuable space in your bathroom.

- Start with the medicine cabinet and work your way through the storage area under the sink. Decide the fate of one item at a time. If you're sure it stays, have part of your temporary work area set aside for each person using this bathroom. Sort the items by type. For example, I had shaving cream and after-shave on Todd's side of my work table. Nail polish and makeup rested comfortably in June's area of the work table.

Slip 'n' Slide Solution

I'm referring to that infamous bathroom drawer you have organized a million times. Each time, you lament that all the order will be destroyed the first time the drawer is closed. I have the solution! Go to the kitchen department of your local hardware or specialty store. You'll find a drawer liner that looks like quilted paper towels. This is a wonderful product that will grip whatever is placed on it. Now the things you place with care will be there when you need them, like faithful soldiers of the bath. Be creative with every solution in this book. Why not line all the problem drawers in your home with this product?

The Underworld

It must be part of Murphy's Law that at least one time during your tenure in your current residence, there will be a plumbing problem and everything will have to be yanked out from under the sink. The plumber will no doubt chastise you for keeping anything in this space. Obviously, he doesn't wear makeup or have to primp! Let's see what we can do to make the removal of the items stored here easy for the plumber and convenient for you in between his house calls.

In the kitchen and bathroom organization areas of your local hardware or specialty store, you will find containers. There are endless varieties, including the following:

- An item called a junior crate, which is a scaled-down version of the large ones found at office supply stores.
- Containers in all shapes and sizes that have lids.
- Two- and three-drawer units, some big enough to be used like a small dresser, others small enough to perch on a counter top.

❧ Small, square containers that would be perfect as a repository for small items, like a lady's scattered bobby pins. These containers come in long versions (just right for manicure accessories) and extra long to house items like combs or toothbrushes. You can use one color for the lady of the house, one color for the man's possessions, and clear acrylic for the items they share.

The list of container types is almost endless. Sort everything in the bathroom and then survey the contents. This will guide you in purchasing the correct storage units. Be sure and measure the space available under the sink before you make a purchase. Some of the larger items are very useful, but the pipes under your sink may interfere. It's easier to remove a storage crate than to scoop out loose items. The plumber will be impressed with your ingenuity.

Imagination at Work

In the kitchen area of your specialty store, you will find a wonderful item used to help you store and display canned goods. It is a shelf creator. Place it on a shelf in your pantry or in a cupboard, and suddenly you have three rows for the display of cans instead of one flat surface with cans lined up, hiding each other's labels. These items now come in narrow and wide to accommodate various sizes of cans on the market. Guess what? You can put these under the sink and store bathroom items.

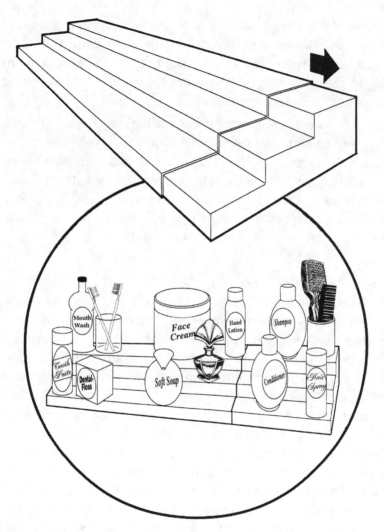

Shelf creator—bathroom.

I want to encourage you as often as possible to see that products made to solve one problem are capable of solving problems in other places in the home. These shelf creators are also wonderful in the laundry room where you probably have several spot removers and other miscellaneous items tucked in with large boxes of detergent. Wouldn't it be nice to see them all at a glance? Are you beginning to see why I think getting organized is a creative endeavor?

Another kitchen item I use in the bathroom is the zip-lock bag. Are you attached to every eyebrow pencil you've ever purchased? Do you take the Q-tips out of their cardboard container and balk at the price of the decorative one in the specialty store? Do you have shampoo containers that leak? A zip-lock bag in a size appropriate for the task is on the market. Again, take this item out of the kitchen and boldly use it elsewhere.

And So It Goes ...

Let's examine the contents of June and Todd's master bathroom so you can see the process involved. I divided things as I went along into his and hers areas of the bathroom. This was a good size room, so I had the luxury of two sinks, two medicine cabinets, and three under-counter storage areas. There were also three drawers on either side I could designate for his and hers articles. Under the center part of the sink area in the middle cabinet, I placed all of the large items that the couple would share. These included extra toilet paper, Q-tips, cotton, shampoo and conditioner, and some basic household items like a drain opener, cleanser, and a sponge for quick cleanups. I used a combination of junior crates and a shelf creator in this space. I like to assemble a first-aid kit for every home so that Band-Aids and the like are in one area for everyone to access as needed. If finances permit, keep first-aid kits in the kitchen and in guest baths as well.

The left side was the area June used. Here we put her cosmetics, hair-care products and tools, feminine hygiene products, and the like. Naturally, we lined the drawers so that items would stay put. I like to place small items that are used frequently in the medicine cabinets. It's nice to keep them at eye level.

I think it is important for the man of the house to have his masculinity honored. Very often husbands will not feel comfortable in a super-feminine, frilly bedroom and bath. I don't blame them. I would be a fish out of water in the black leather, dark wood, chrome and glass domain of most bachelors. June honored Todd, and every room in their home reflected this balance. The opposite side of the long bathroom counter was, therefore, the male domain. In Todd's medicine cabinet, we put his daily-use items like over-the-counter pain relievers and his contact lens saline solution bottles. We also utilized his column of drawers and the area under his personal sink so that they housed only the products he used. For example, the top drawer had his shaving supplies, while another held his dental products.

June and I agreed the counter was to be kept as clear as possible, so we placed beautiful soap dishes on each side and a pretty tissue dispenser in the middle. Some people like more on the counter and, if you have the space, I encourage you to use coordinated containers. It's also helpful to place counter items on a tray so that they have a restricted area in which to live.

Under their individual sink or tucked into their designated drawers, I stored large items and backup supplies for June and Todd's personal needs. Here is where your containers will once again come in handy. Suppose, for instance, you have basic makeup supplies that you use every day. One option is to place these in a drawer on the liner we previously discussed. It might be more efficient to use the drawer liner in concert with an appropriately sized small container to hold these items. Like most women, you probably have seasonal changes in makeup and/or things you only use for special occasions. Your crate or closed container can store all these items and keep them under the sink. I'm thinking of wonderful items like holiday glitter for hair or soft pastel lipsticks that complement a summer sun tan. There are specific times of the year these treasures are in vogue. I'm not empowered in any way if I have to see or handle them on a daily basis. When you want more than the basics, they'll be waiting neatly in one area. You will have avoided rummaging through everything you own in the morning before you go to the office where, I presume, glitter is generally frowned upon.

Here's another example of storing related items in different ways. June liked to have a set of hot rollers on the counter. At five every morning, she didn't want to have to reach for them under the sink. They could be plugged in as she jumped into the shower. Like most women who use rollers, she had multiple sets with roller sizes for special occasions. We did store these under the sink, as they were scheduled for guest appearances only.

Bathroom Checklist

Here's a list of additional things you can do to help turn your bathroom into a safe haven. Pick and choose depending on your current bathroom size. Don't forget to tuck ideas away for your future bathroom.

- ☐ Are the walls painted a pretty color? Would a special technique like sponge painting add interest to the room or perhaps to just one wall?
- ☐ Is there an outside window? Make a trip to your local nursery and investigate the plants that would thrive under the light and humidity conditions in your bathroom. No window? Bring in some silk flowers.

☐ If your budget permits, be creative with the towels, the rugs, and the shower curtain. Consider seasonal changes of these items.

☐ Don't ignore the soap dish or dispenser, the tissue holder, the toothbrush holder, and so on. These add personality as well as function to the room.

☐ Make this a room that always smells good by burning scented candles or putting potpourri in decorative containers.

☐ If you have multiple bathrooms, decorate each one with a different theme. You can have elegant accessories in the master, for example, and be whimsical in the guest bath.

☐ Hang pictures on the walls or items from collections someone in the house has started.

☐ If you are so inclined, keep reading matter handy.

☐ Short on space? Hang a shelf or install a cabinet.

☐ Hair flics in a bathroom and it's nice to do daily touchups of the area. I would strongly suggest keeping a dust buster handy. Cat owners will frequently place a kitty litter box in the bathroom. What can be more annoying than jumping out of a shower and stepping on stray kitty gravel? Your dust buster will serve you here as well.

☐ If the room is small, look elsewhere to store your entire selection of towels or all the toilet paper you buy. I had a client who had more shirts than the local department store. He and his wife had very few towel sets. We used the linen closet to store his shirts. Get the idea?

The Postage Stamp Bathroom

Dale lives in a tiny apartment near the ocean in a Southern California beach community. In exchange for large rooms, she has clean air to breathe year round, the smell of the ocean from the minute she wakes up, and the sound of the sea gulls. If she gained as little as eight ounces on her tiny frame, however, she would not be able to turn around in her bathroom.

She has one small medicine cabinet on the wall and absolutely no room for any other type of storage. Getting dressed in the morning is problematic, as she has no game plan. She begins her day not only with the frustration inherent in her situation, but with tremendous resentment that this seems to be a setup with no solution.

Miraculously, just outside the bathroom in her bedroom, a storage unit had been cut into the wall. It served as a small linen closet. I immediately cleaned out a dresser drawer for her linens and used these shelves for her grooming aids and toiletries. Each category was placed into a container. When she was ready for her makeup, she brought out that container and placed it on her closed toilet seat cover. She would replace this with the hair accoutrements container and so on.

Had Dale not had these shelves, I would have suggested she purchase an inexpensive three-drawer plastic unit that rolls. It could be tucked into a corner of her bedroom and wheeled to the doorway of the bathroom every morning. As long as every item she needed was in one place, she'd be in the control position.

As you can see, the size of your bathroom does not matter, nor do the number of items you feel are necessary to deal with in order to be ready for presentation to the world. You are limited only by the creative use of your imagination in solving the problems at hand.

Crate O' My Heart

I don't believe that intimacy is enhanced when we throw our possessions together in a physical mish-mash designed to fray nerves. I have a client who is very neat and tidy by nature. He loved the idea of putting his everyday toilet items into a small crate that he stores under the sink. He places it on the counter when he needs to prepare for the day. Before he leaves for work, he returns the container to its position under the sink. On the counter he has a display of beautiful bottles. This area is very inviting now and easy to maintain. When we first met, it looked like a small cyclone had passed through. John had no idea there was a way to avoid clutter and still find what you needed when you wanted it. And there was one additional complication.

His sweetheart lives part of the year in another city. Unlike John, she does not mind being surrounded by a sea of bottles, brushes, and tubes. We introduced her to the crate concept and, as a compromise, she has decided to make use of one as well. Now her things reside in a quiet corner of the cabinet under the sink, rather than spreading across the counter like a fungus. She can retrieve them easily whenever she is in residence. When she is away, they live quietly under the sink in one controlled area waiting for her return. John meanwhile is soothed by the absence of clutter.

"I Don't Know Where This Goes …"

The very first time you pick up an item, shrug your shoulders, say to yourself "I don't know where this goes," and toss it on the counter or in a drawer, you have jeopardized all your efforts at organizing this room. One casually tossed item will call to its brethren and, before you can invoke the name *The Zen of Organizing*, bottles, jars, and brushes will have bled across the nicely organized space like ooze in a horror movie. You are creating the system. You determine the placement of everything you own.

Final Note

Cleansing and dressing the body should be sacred tasks. The soul is eternal. The body it resides in deserves a place to rest and restore itself. This body is a gift from our Creator. In the bathroom, we are given a special opportunity to honor it.

寿

Long Life

CHAPTER 6

Kitchens

*"Do you know that you are God's temple
and that God's spirit dwells in you?
For God's temple is holy,
and that temple you are."*

—*1 Corinthians*

One day I was called to organize a closet in the guest room of a big house not far from Los Angeles. As frequently happens, we soon embarked on the task of organizing every nook and cranny. I was surprised when my client Marian said she was a gourmet cook. During our telephone chat, she had mentioned that she rarely prepared a meal in her kitchen. My Sherlock Holmes hat goes on when I hear conflicting comments like this. I am immediately in quest of the reason and the solution.

The Haunted Cupboards

It struck me that Marian might be delusional about the quality of her cooking until we began to empty and identify the contents of the cupboards. Her husband had been married once before and had lived with his first wife in this house. What should we find buried in the upper reaches of the tallest shelves but items belonging to his former wife. Deeper excavation unearthed even more treasures: cooking items belonging to a previous live-in girlfriend. I told Marian she needed to deep-six these items immediately. Like the grunions rotting in my friend's glove compartment, *people's possessions affect our environment. It's like leaving an "energetic scent" behind you.* Desmond Morris says humans mark territory with their possessions just like animals do in the wild with their body fluids. We carefully removed those unwanted items from their hiding places. Later I was not at all surprised to learn that Marian had begun cooking up a storm.

Where Does It Go?

Of all the tasks I perform as a professional organizer, the one I love above all the others is unpacking a new home. However, inevitably, I will be asked some variation of this question: "If you unpack me, how will I know where anything is?" I am always struck by the fear this represents. It is as if people imagine that I will put their toothbrush in the pantry, the iron under the bed, and their clothing in the garage just to see how confused I can make them. If you stop and look objectively at any house or apartment, you can see that a logical place for everything already exists. Let's take a look at the kitchen from this perspective. As we go along, I'll give you organizing tips to make your kitchen a more pleasurable place to spend time in. After all, don't we always seem to wind up in this room?

Blueprint for the American Kitchen

Walk into any kitchen in America and you'll find cabinets above the sink. On one side, you'll discover the everyday dishes; on the other side, you'll see the drinking glasses. Open a drawer in this vicinity and you'll spy a cutlery tray filled with the silverware. Oh yes, the pot holders live on or near the stove. See what I mean?

In California just about everyone has a small pantry for their food. Growing up in a Brooklyn brownstone, we stored food in the cupboards and in a separate piece of furniture that served as a pantry. Chaos creeps in with the remaining items you want to have in your kitchen. It's as if the "Let's just stick it here" fairies rule.

In large kitchens you have the luxury of multiple cupboards near the sink, a cooking island with storage space underneath it, and additional cupboards under counters across the room. Some of my clients have kitchens that are bigger than apartments I rented in New York City! Once I lived in a studio apartment in Brooklyn Heights. The kitchen (I use the term loosely) had a small stove, a small sink, and (what else?) a small refrigerator. (I believe Gulliver stopped here in his travels.) I had two cabinets above the sink and an area underneath. The kitchen was closed off with a sliding door. It was a place only someone in their 20s could endure. Needless to say, in a tiny corner like this, you aren't going to have a state-of-the-art food processor on the counter (what counter?) or an elaborate cache of expensive pots and pans because you'd have to stack them on the day bed and move them when you wanted to go to sleep. I'm going to describe the placement of kitchen items in what would undeniably be a good-size room. If you have a matchbox kitchen, follow the general principles.

Command Stations

Imagine a busy day in the ER of a big city hospital. What would happen if the exam rooms had not been stocked? What if the supplies available had been placed helter-skelter in each room? Now unless you are related to *Sweeney Todd,* we obviously won't be losing any lives in your kitchen. You will, however, be in a constant state of irritation if a minor drama ensues every time you want to cook or bake.

The tasks performed in a kitchen are as follows:

* Cooking
* Baking
* Eating
* Food storage

Since we can so easily identify specific tasks, why not divide kitchen equipment and gadgets by task and store them in specific areas? It could be accomplished like this:

* In one area, located as close as possible to the sink, will be all of the food preparation items you need. This includes tools like a food processor, your favorite bowl, and a salad spinner.

* Near the stove, you'll want to find your pots and pans. I like to keep pots and their lids together. If space does not permit this, stacking the pieces is my *second* choice. You can purchase holders for the lids and a divider for any trays you might have. You have to judge the space and see if the extra pieces are a hindrance or a help.

* Baking has evolved into a special occasion for me, so I don't mind if baking items are not in the area immediately adjacent to the sink. If you're a stay-at-home parent who bakes cookies and bread on a daily basis, you may want closer proximity to the sink. In either event, be sure all your baking supplies stay together.

* The dishes, glasses, silverware, napkins, and place mats are organized so that the actual task of setting the table will be speedy and enjoyable. In other words, they, too, are in one *established* area. We know the first three have traditional places to occupy. Napkins and placements should be in a drawer closest to the table or counter

where you will be dining. *You want to plot your command stations in a logical flow of energy consumption.* If the place mats, as an example, are stored at the opposite end of the kitchen from the eating area, you are wasting steps. Wasted steps equal wasted time. Redeem all this wasted time, and you will have enough time to write the great American novel, run for president of the United States, or perhaps just live a more balanced life. Direct your life force; don't squander it.

✻ Don't forget to establish a home for containers and other food storage items. What can be more wasteful than walking in circles looking for foil in one area and those infamous plastic storage containers in another? Avoid setting up the kitchen in a way that finds you constantly muttering under your breath, "I can never find anything in this kitchen!"

✻ Store small tools in drawers in related clusters. You don't want to be confronted by a rolling pin, a knife sharpener, and a tea ball in the same place. If you are blessed with enough drawers, keep baking items together, cooking utensils in another, and specialty items like that pizza cutter in a third.

✻ Lots of cooks like a container on the counter that houses the most frequently used tools. If you have the counter space, use an attractive container. Less frequently used tools can happily reside in the drawer.

✻ Don't forget to use drawer liner to prevent slip 'n' slide. In addition, you may want to use small containers in varying sizes to house your tools. We wouldn't want to carefully divide everything and then discover a chaotic mess was forming in the drawer.

Withering Heights

I have lost track of the number of tiny clients who peer into a cabinet I have just organized and inform me that there is no way they can possibly access the top shelf. I tend to forget that everyone is not at least 5'9".

The top shelves in any of your cupboards afford you invaluable space. You'll want to take advantage and, fortunately, a simple solution is at hand. There are one-step stools available that can be left in the kitchen for your convenience. Some fold up and can be tucked into an open slot between appliances. The ones that do not fold work best in large kitchens where they can be left in a corner or placed under the bottom shelf in the pantry. If you are tiny, consider placing a step stool in other areas of the house where easy access to high shelves is important.

Food Storage

I love the pantry. There is something incredibly nurturing about walking into a space devoted to the storage of food. Inevitably, these sweet spaces have every manner of food hurled onto their shelves with no rhyme or reason. Let's look at food the way we looked at clothing. It makes sense to put all of your skirts or all of your slacks in one section, right? Let's create food categories and group the cans, bottles, and bags as well. Not only will you be able to find what you need easily, you'll know when you're running short.

Some of the most common food groups include the following:

- Grains and pasta
- Vegetables (canned)

- Fruits (canned)
- Cereals
- Desserts and snacks
- Soups
- Main dishes in cans (such as tuna)
- Soft drinks
- Juices
- Coffee, teas, and their partners (artificial sweeteners, honey, and so on)
- Baking items (flours, sugar, and so on)

How will you keep order after you physically divide the contents into specific areas on the shelves?

- Remember the shelf dividers we used in the closet to separate your sweaters? If your pantry shelves aren't too thick, those dividers will work nicely here as well.
- Please consider putting labels on the shelves. I also label the drawers and all the cabinets. This is especially helpful if you live with a large number of people.
- The shelf creators we used in the bathroom were actually designed for the storage of canned foods. They come in various widths to accommodate the variety of can sizes on the market. You'll be able to see three rows of cans at a glance instead of guessing what you stashed in the back of the shelf.

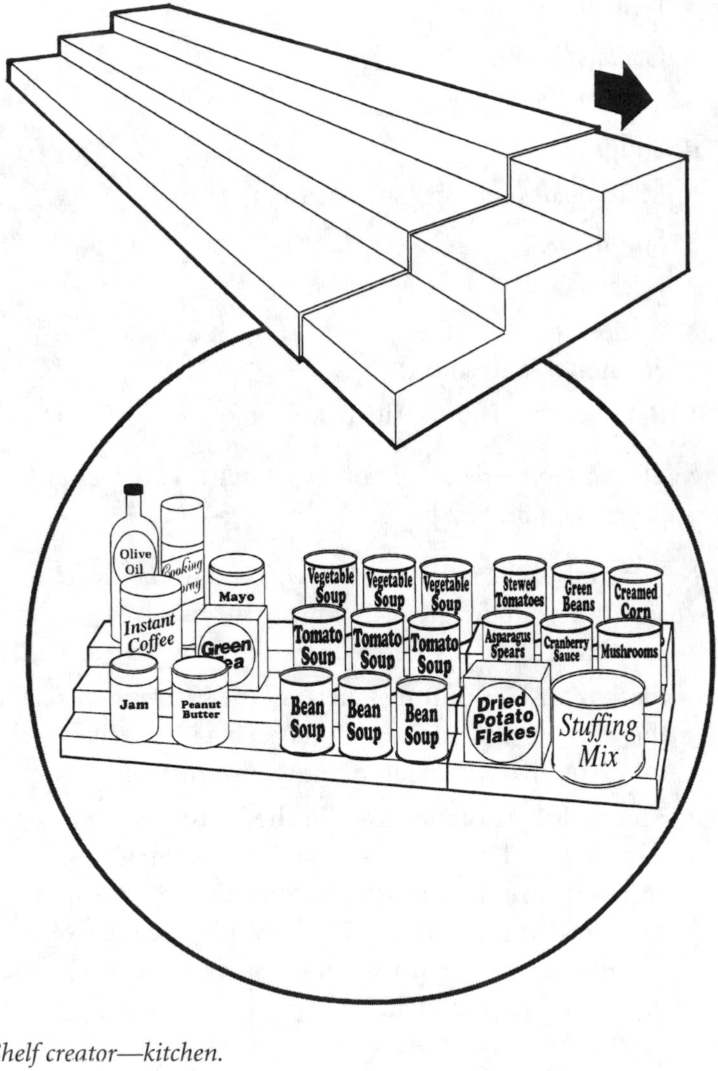

Shelf creator—kitchen.

- I use shelf creators in a large pantry in addition to shelf baskets designed for this express purpose. Unlike ordinary baskets, they dip in front so you can easily reach in and take out the onion or potato you need.

- Whenever possible, discard packaging.

- Do you have pets? I store my Golden Retriever's dog biscuits in glass jars to keep them fresh and away from any creatures that might be drawn to them. Keep your cans of dog and cat food in one area, neatly stacked by type. If you feed your pet kibble, store the food in a large plastic container.

- It's a good idea to keep all loose foods sealed in plastic zip-lock bags or in glass containers. Candidates include open bags of pretzels, cookies, or crackers. Bag clips are a second choice in my mind as they do not ensure freshness.

- Vegetarians, like myself, are frequently beset by moth-like creatures that grow in some grains. This problem can be avoided if you store all grains in glass containers. It's a shock the first time you encounter these creatures, and it takes quite a bit of effort to get rid of them.

- If you're a big consumer of canned beverages, there are special containers for storing cans that dispense them one at a time. These dispensers can be placed in the pantry or in the refrigerator depending on the size of both areas and the frequency of consumption.

The Macho Drawer

Every kitchen has one drawer I have dubbed the "macho drawer." Here you will find a screwdriver, perhaps a small hammer, some picture hooks or nails, and so on. We all seem to need these items close at hand. There are wonderful multi-sectioned plastic containers aimed at tidying this drawer and its complement of tiny treasures. You can purchase such an organizer or you can use some food storage bags. The important thing is for all the small items like nails to be in one spot should you ever need one. In any event, do line the drawer. Keep the macho supplies to a minimum and store them low to the ground in one of the deep bottom drawers. If you have room for a small toolbox in the pantry, you might free this drawer completely.

The Junk Drawer

Let's be honest. You have a junk drawer, don't you? Everybody has a drawer near the phone that has paper, pens, paper clips, and whatever miscellaneous items their family feels they need. I never take this drawer away from a client. I do put in drawer liner and perhaps some small containers. These work well to hold things like writing implements and miscellaneous office supplies. Trash what you don't need. Transport what does not belong to a more appropriate space. Batteries are usually found rolling around in this drawer. They last longer stored in the refrigerator.

The Neighbors

Here I'm referring to all the other drawers in your kitchen. We discussed sorting the cooking tools. We noted the traditional placement of the silverware. Kitchen supplies like tea towels, place mats, and napkins you use on a daily basis need to be kept handy, as we also noted. If you have a linen closet nearby, store the bulk of them there and keep exactly the number you do use in each category in the kitchen. Consider using space in the laundry room for the backup supplies we inevitably purchase if the pantry is full of food. Here we're considering the extra food storage bags, paper napkins, garbage bags, paper towels, and the like.

Counter Wars

My clients are divided into two camps when it comes to the counter space in their kitchen. Most like the counter completely clear. The other group likes to see every kitchen gadget they've ever purchased out and ready for action. I vote for the middle ground. If you use a piece of equipment frequently, like a coffee-maker every morning, keep it out. Why waste time hauling it out and putting it away? On the other hand, if your food processor is for holiday food preparation only, find a home hidden below.

Remember, too, that items on top of the counter can be clustered in categories relative to their function. For example, in the morning you might want toast and coffee. Your coffee-maker and your toaster will make lovely companions near one of the outlets. If you are a busy mom who cooks every night, the blender, the mini processor, and the electric can opener are candidates for another cluster around an outlet.

Spices

You may find that alphabetizing your spices will make cooking a little easier.

Here are some spice storage ideas:

- ❧ I like two-tier turntables for spices. They tuck nicely into cupboards.
- ❧ Spice holders that can attach to a cabinet and be pulled down when you need them work well.
- ❧ In a drawer, you can insert spice holders that enable you to lay the bottles down for easy viewing.
- ❧ Some clients have extremely deep drawers and place the spices here in the upright position. I make labels for the jar tops and make sure they are in alphabetical order.

These drawers usually have dividers you can insert. This way a controlled number of spices live in small areas within the space of the entire drawer.

- There are some really beautiful high-tech containers that are designed to sit on the counter.
- If you aren't a big cook and have only the bare necessities in spices, try a shelf creator in a cupboard near your cooking area.

The solution depends on how many spices you have, how often you use them, and where your kitchen allows you to store them.

In summary, what are the most common counter items?

- Breakfast prep items
- Food prep items
- Mail basket
- Canisters
- Specialty items too large to store, such as large espresso/cappuccino machines
- Spice rack
- Paper towel dispenser (mounted versions work better)

The Cave of Chaos

Just about every home I've ever organized has had a frightening mess under the sink. It's somewhat amusing to me to see a beautifully setup kitchen secretly harboring this cave of chaos. Remember, we're trying to create a room whose elements work totally in concert. *As each room follows this pattern, the home itself becomes a physical expression of the peace and calm we hope to experience within.*

Here are some tips to bring your cave into alignment with the order you're creating in the rest of the room:

- ❧ Start by tossing away the half-empty cans that live there. Combine the contents of multiple half-empty containers.

- ❧ You need to put all of your supplies in categories (cleaning versus polishing versus everyday-use products) and, of course, you'll want to pop them into containers.

- ❧ Cleaning supply caddies are helpful. You can easily take products with you as you tackle cleaning projects around the house.

- ❧ If your pipes allow, there are stackable shelves. Each slides for ease in retrieving the everyday supplies. You might want to combine solutions depending on the size of the area in question.

- ❧ Try and keep your backup cleaning supplies in one area. In a large house with a separate laundry room, I suggest you store the backup cleaning supplies in that room. I think the rule of "one in use and one as a backup" works for most things. When you go to your command station to restock, you'll automatically know when it's time to add an item to your grocery list. You can also check it off the master list I suggested in Chapter 2, "Time."

Creating Atmosphere

I love plants and think they are a positive addition to every room. If you have the counter space and a window, do add a bit of life and personality with a plant. Can't remember to water them? I'll bet you have a calendar by now with your schedule kept up to date in its pages. Once a week, note "water plants." The rewards are many. Plants not only look beautiful, but they clean the air of pollutants and give oxygen to the atmosphere. There are varieties you would be hard-pressed to kill. Talk with your local nursery about the hardy varieties that will survive in the environment you offer.

A wonderful way to set the mood in a kitchen is with lighting. Place a small lamp on your counter if space allows. In the morning, as we prepare for the day, we like a bright, cheery kitchen. The evening meal is probably a time of lively interaction if you're a large family. Those late-night forays to the kitchen for a snack or a beverage, however, can be made in the gentle, quiet light of a lamp. My clients listen to this idea and are generally unimpressed. I ask if I can try a lamp just to see how it looks. Inevitably, they become converts. I hope you'll give it a chance. No counter space? Try a dimmer switch.

Miscellaneous Notes

* Many people store wine in the kitchen. If your supply is limited to a few bottles and you have the space, purchase a pretty wine rack. If the wine is expensive and the rack is a work of art, move the unit into the dining room.

* I like to keep the top of the refrigerator clear. I do think, however, that a modest display of cookbooks can be quite attractive. Keeping them at arms reach for the cook increases the likelihood of tasty treats making an appearance. Be sure and use bookends.

* Try making a visually inviting display of your dishes, such as the following:

    * There are individual dish display stands in the kitchen area of your local specialty or hardware store. Set off a pretty platter. Display that antique dish you'll never eat off. One client had beautiful blue dishes hidden on the shelf with his everyday

set. I put two of them on stands so that they were visible in the glass panes on the cupboard door. It turned out these dishes were antiques from Eastern Europe. Walter had purchased them on a trip to Bulgaria for his wife. My clients had never thought to use a dish display holder. Now everyone gets to enjoy these beautiful dishes with an ancient past.

- You can also prop some of the serving dishes against the back wall of the cupboard. My clients love this look and often marvel saying, "I never would have thought to do that, and it's so pretty!"

- There are plastic dish stands you place in the corner of a cupboard that enable you to separate a stack of dishes by type. This automatically creates more shelf space.

- Be creative with your glass display as well. For example, if you have glass panes on your cabinets, display some of the pretty ones on the second shelf and keep the "grab every day" ones on the bottom.

- If you have the space under a cabinet, you can install a rack that will enable you to hang your wine glasses.

- Consider changing the decorative items in your kitchen with the seasons. These include tea towels, pot holders, your aprons, or some decorative items like fake pumpkins at Halloween.

The Chef with Bare Cupboards

If I am asked to organize the entire home, I like to tour it before I begin work. One day a famous chef asked me to organize his Beverly Hills condo. The closets were jammed with clothes and other possessions. It would take a few days of work and shopping to restore order. When I headed for the kitchen, he told me there was nothing to organize. I had to see it with my own eyes. He wasn't kidding. There were a few dishes and a single set of everyday silverware. I think I recall a coffeemaker. There was no food. The cupboards were indeed bare. He said he ate breakfast out and had his other meals at the restaurant. I thought how ironic it was that people traveled from all over LA to sample his food and he never cooked for himself at home. Whenever I see him on TV, I always chuckle inside about the secret we share.

I encouraged him, by the way, to keep *some* food in those cupboards. On a rainy night when you or your best buddy want a snack, I hate to think of you staring into a barren cupboard while your stomachs growl world-class renditions of "Yankee Doodle Dandy."

The kitchen represents one of the key means at our disposal to nurture ourselves, our family members, and our guests. I invite you to take advantage of the opportunity this represents. Even if you, too, own a famous Beverly Hills eatery!

Final Note

My goal in this chapter has been to help you create an environment that continues the flow of peace and calm you are establishing in your home. From the moment you wake up in the morning, you want every facet of your environment working with you, not against you. As you do the work indicated in previous chapters and begin to bathe and dress in comfort and ease, you will want to continue those good feelings with your organized, harmonious kitchen.

Love

CHAPTER 7

The Common Rooms

*"Do not neglect to show
hospitality to strangers,
for thereby some have
entertained angels unaware."*

—Hebrews 13:2

As I began to work on this chapter, I was house-sitting for a friend. I always feel like I'm on vacation when I go there. The decorating theme is the American cowboy. For a girl from Brooklyn, having Buffalo Bill in the bathroom is wild indeed! Cowboys are everywhere. They adorn the lampshades. They are painted on the kitchen dishes. I can grab a cowboy hat and sit on cowhide in two shakes of a lamb's tail. Or should I say "horse's tail"?

Setting the Stage

My favorite room in my friend's house is the office. It was added on after the original structure was built and it isn't insulated. On chilly winter mornings, my friend builds a fire in the stove and in minutes the room is toasty warm. Sitting at the computer, you look out onto a beautiful garden. It's feels like a mini-vacation in the mountains without ever leaving Los Angeles.

What does all this have to do with organizing the common rooms? When we decorate a room, we are really doing two things at once:

- ♠ We express a part of our personality.
- ♠ We create a comfort zone for guests and family members.

Take a minute to walk into *your* living room. Let's pretend that you don't live there. For our purposes, this is now the set for a TV show. List three things you immediately know about the main character.

My friend's home, for instance, yields these clues about its occupant:

- ♠ He loves the western heritage of the United States.
- ♠ I gather he has a strong sense of family because pictures are everywhere.
- ♠ The couch is comfortable and there is a big easy chair. This tells me he likes to have people come over and sit down with him.
- ♠ The coffee table is very large. It can accommodate food, drinking glasses, magazines, and so on. Again, an interest in entertaining is evident.
- ♠ There is a piano, and I see sheet music is out. Someone in this house must enjoy playing.
- ♠ As a dog owner, I notice that the couch has a cover on the seat. This tells me that the house is animal-friendly.
- ♠ I also spy a basket of dog toys.

I am aware of these things without a word being spoken. After you decide what you know about the occupant of the room you're in, ask yourself if this person likes having other people around. Do you feel embraced and welcomed by the surroundings? Or do you get the idea that it would be best not to settle in for a long visit? *Let's make it our shared goal to reveal how much we respect and care for all those with whom we share our common rooms. We can start by getting control over the specific items we find here.*

Music: The World of Records, CDs, and Cassette Tapes

I have always been amused to note that even the poorest guy will have a stereo system. My wealthy male clients often have their sound technicians show up before the moving truck pulls out of the driveway. Men usually have fairly complicated organizing systems for their records, CDs, and tapes. If you have such a male in your home, let him take the reins on this project. Or you might ask a male friend what kind of system he created and borrow some of his ideas.

For the neophyte, here are a few sound ideas to help you get control of this very important element of life. After all, it is music that calms us, inspires us, entertains us, and even soothes the savage beast in us.

- ♣ If you are a patient and meticulous person, put everything in alphabetical order, either by title, composer, or performer.

- ♣ Should you be so inclined, make a master computer list of everything you own. This is invaluable if you have multiple dwellings and wonder if you have a particular musical recording and need to know where it resides. Either you or a staff person must be responsible for keeping the list up-to-date. Depending on the value of the collection, this is also a good tool for insurance purposes.

&. If you are of "a certain age," you may have a record collection. Since I still have most of the albums I grew up with, I would never ask you to toss yours. If you no longer play them, however, consider storing them in a place where they will be safe. You don't want them damaged by humidity or excessive heat, nor do you want to place anything heavy on the boxes that hold them. There are, by the way, special boxes designed for this purpose. Putting the physical record away doesn't mean you have to be robbed of its music. You can now transfer it to cassette. If the original record is badly scratched, consider tossing it as the listening pleasure has been diminished.

&. No matter what source (record, cassette, or CD) you rely on for your listening pleasure, the best way to keep track of everything is to divide the collection first into different types of music. Basic suggestions include the following:

&. Rock, alternative rock

&. Hip-hop and rap

&. Jazz

&. Country/western

&. Broadway

&. Classical/opera

&. Big band/orchestral and so on

Once the categories have been separated out, you can further refine them in this way:

&. Male versus female vocalists

&. Specific groups (Baby boomers always have their Beatles albums in one place!)

&. Italian, French, or German operas (Puccini and Wagner probably don't want to sit together.)

- ❧ Broadway musicals separated by decade or composer (Rogers and Hammerstein in one corner, Sondheim in the other!)
- ❧ Classical music could be divided by composer or era

It's really all about playing with your collection and reducing it to categories that are familiar and comfortable for you personally. Keeping the smaller categories in alphabetical order is a matter of taste and personality. Whatever floats your boat, in this instance, is the correct thing to do. Factors like how often you play music and how many different personalities touch the items must be considered as well. Most teenagers wouldn't be interested in the opera/classical music section of the collection. If the adult who loves this music wants it in alphabetical order, so be it. You'll be lucky to get most children and teenagers to honor the categories. But let's not push the issue. Listening to music should be an enjoyable experience, not a new route to family discord.

- ❧ If you have entertainment centers in more than one area of the house, try and divide the collections with an eye to where the type of music in question is listened to. I have clients who own a large estate with a main residence and a guesthouse among the structures on the property. The guesthouse is used for casual parties, and you'll find most of the dance music stored here. In the main house's living room, you'll find the children's entertainment choices. The parents keep the big band and classical music in their master suite. You get the idea.
- ❧ There are containers made for the express purpose of keeping cassettes, CDs and VHS tapes in order:
  - ❧ You can use the fancy ones for the items you want on display in the room at all times. My favorite is a

lizard crawling up the wall that holds CDs in his back.

&. The more casual containers work well inside the cupboards of an entertainment center. I like the acrylic ones best.

&. If funds permit, a carpenter can build storage compartments into the drawers of this unit.

&. Have you lost the containers your cassettes and tapes were sold in? Plain ones are available at your audio/ video store. Respect your possessions, and you will enjoy them for years to come.

&. Do you live in a postage-stamp-size apartment? Research some catalogues, then shop in stores to see what furniture is available for multiple purposes in the home. For example, you might want to put a CD storage unit on the wall that looks like a piece of sculpture. Or you might want to hide some of your cassette collection in a small unit that can double as an end table by the couch. Limited space requires creative solutions. It also demands being ruthless about what is absolutely needed.

Windows to the Soul

Every now and then I walk into a home that seems to lack something. It takes me a while to realize exactly what is missing. "A house without books is like a house without windows." I do hope you have books in your home and that you treasure them. Most of my clients place their books around the house on various bookcases without rhyme or reason. I like to follow the basic principles we used in sorting our music collection. To wit ...

❧ Divide the collection so that books are strategically placed around the house. Keep specific genres closest to the person who will most enjoy them. Here are some examples:

  ❧ I prefer biography, spiritual, and self-help books and like to keep these in my bedroom.

  ❧ Reference books stay in my office. I wouldn't expect to find my guests browsing through the latest in organizing books when they come for dinner.

  ❧ When I had a country house, I kept novels in the guestroom.

  ❧ Cookbooks generally reside in the kitchen.

  ❧ If dad likes to tinker in the garage working on cars or refinishing furniture, why not create a reference shelf there to help support his efforts?

  ❧ Categorize books before you place them on shelves. Why have your collection of history books scattered on the shelves of a bookcase or, worse, scattered throughout the house? When you wonder where a particular book is located, you'll have only to remember where you parked that category.

❧ My mother taught me a great visual trick to make a bookcase more interesting and inviting. Instead of lining all the books up like soldiers on every shelf, create a varied pattern. A few books can be stacked on the end of a shelf. You can vary the corner you decide to stack: left to start and then right a few shelves down. Collectibles or plants can be interspersed throughout. Make the visual not only interesting, but restful to the eye.

Bookcase.

- 🍂 I prefer not to alphabetize my books. The shapes vary and the result can be visually disturbing. Remember that your current living space may one day no longer accommodate your growing collection. I'm sure a book or two could be donated to charity the day you send over those clothes you've decided you're not going to wear again.

- 🍂 Be sure and give special attention to the more expensive volumes you own. You can purchase clear jackets to keep them protected from things like dust and sticky fingers.

- 🍂 A large collection can be logged in to the computer with a code as to the book's whereabouts. For example, *The*

Zen of Organizing, followed by DL/N could mean "Downstairs Library, Nonfiction." Here is where your personal creativity comes into play. Have fun creating these systems. And remember, they aren't set in stone. You can change them every few years if you like.

Movie Magic

We all do it. We record endless hours of television programs because we're sure that one day we'll settle down and get caught up. What to do with all these tapes? The solutions mirror the ones we used for music and books. Let's consider a few possibilities:

- Separate tapes purchased from tapes recorded at home.
- Keep the pre-recorded tapes in categories so you can easily enjoy them with family and friends. What are movie categories? I use the following:
  - Action
  - Musical
  - Drama
  - Comedy
  - Sports/exercise
  - Children/animated
- The retrieval system you create should be easy to maintain and function without stress. If space allows, physically separate the categories in different sections of the entertainment unit. You can also use VHS tape holders to keep the categories separate and neat. Once again, I am partial to the acrylic holders.
- Place all family tapes in a special area and be sure they are clearly labeled. You don't want to erase your baby's

first birthday celebration by mistake one day when you're reaching for a tape to record your favorite soap opera.

❧ Every house I go to has at least 10 tapes that are "mystery guests." No one would think of using them because a piece of gold was probably recorded on one of them. By the same token, no one ever makes the time to view them and solve the mystery. The key to keeping control over personally recorded tapes is to label them immediately. If you are part of a large household, I would also separate tapes by owner. Mom's soap opera tapes will be of no interest to Junior who cherishes his basketball tapes. If they are not separated and labeled, however, mother and son are setting themselves up for an accidental use that can cause hard feelings.

Photo Albums

Just about every client I work with has boxes of photographs hidden away in a closet or attic. They wait patiently for some future rainy day when a photo project will occupy their time. And just about everyone gets apoplectic at the very idea of dealing with their photos. What's a person to do? Putting together a beautiful photo album takes time, but is worth the effort. Let's look at a few things you can do to take control of this area:

❧ While waiting for that rainy day, be sure you have a system for handling all the photos that come into your home from this day forward. It can be as simple as purchasing photo boxes and carefully labeling the individual photo packets when you pick them up at the store.

- Take a class in creating interesting albums at your local community college. You may currently be unmotivated because you see no way to enjoy the process.

- If you have a large workroom devoted to projects of this nature, you have struck pay dirt. If not, an extra shelf can be added to most closets. This can be an ideal spot to stash your project in between work sessions. You don't want to create a drama every time you decide to work on the album. Everything should be kept in one area.

- Display your albums on the coffee table in your living room. After you have several completed, you can rotate them. Is there a wedding coming up in your family? Put your wedding album out while the upcoming event is on everyone's mind. Is it holiday time? Take out the pictorial record of holidays past to share with family and friends. Was your family vacation a safari to Africa this year? I can't imagine anyone not wanting to see those photos. You get the idea.

- Give albums to your children as they leave home to establish their adult lives. Tell them it's now up to them to document their future so that one day their children will have a strong sense of their immediate family history. This pictorial genealogy should inspire generations to come.

- I like to see smaller items incorporated into photo albums to add interest. For example, cards you have received from someone mixed in with photos of them create visual interest on the page. It allows the person to come alive for those who have never had an opportunity to meet them.

The Perpetual Odd Couple

If one person in a relationship tends to be a pack rat, the other will be virtually ruthless about creating order in the environment. It never fails. It is as if God is balancing the scales. One year I did some projects for just such a couple. He had absolutely no concept about how to manage his environment. His problem wasn't a lack of intelligence; it was a total lack of interest. In his business, he surrounded himself with organized people who kept paper trails for him. At home, he lived with a Martha Stewart clone.

One of the last projects I did for this couple was preparing the family photo collection for a professional archivist. This archivist was hired to come in and create the actual albums. My task was to devise a system that would make her work easier. I was presented with several large boxes of photos. In years past, another organizer had made the following divisions:

- A box for each of the five children
- A box with the courtship and pre-children photos
- Several boxes of memorabilia from parties and childhood events

After careful consideration, I came up with a plan. It would be nice to create multiple albums from the photos in each category. Each child would be given a pictorial record of his years at home. Although the album would be primarily a personal record, there would be equal time for one's siblings. Actually, so many photos had been developed, an album for the parents was also planned. The age of multiple copies has its advantages. For each child, I made the following categories:

- Baby pictures
- Toddler years
- Pre-school

- Elementary school
- Middle school
- High school
- College
- Parties
- Special interests

I purchased several boxes of sheet protectors at the stationery store that are specifically designed to house photos. I made labels for each of these categories. The photos were then sorted on a table and placed in the appropriate jacket. The last thing I did was to buy file boxes for each child and make labels that corresponded to these categories.

After the initial album is completed, suppose Aunt Tilly is visiting and asks to see what the archivist has created. "Oh!" exclaims Tilly, "I simply must have a copy of this photo of Tony in his riding britches when he was five years old." Mom would go to the storage area upstairs where the photos were kept. Out would come Tony's box. Inside she would check the sheet protector marked "toddler." If an extra photo existed, Aunt Tilly could receive instant gratification. Negatives should also be clearly marked and filed appropriately. Aunt Tilly might have to wait for that treasured copy.

Labor Day Weekend

Of course, not every family has as many photos or the vast resources to make perfect albums. I've shared this story to spark your creativity. When I moved to California, I, too, had a box of photos. I grew up with them. One September I decided to make albums. I sorted for the entire weekend. Thank goodness my Golden Retriever hadn't entered my life as yet. Katie hates projects that encroach on her territory.

I made two albums. One chronicled my parents' courtship and my life from birth to college graduation. The second started the pictorial record of my adult-life adventures and friends. Now when friends ask questions about my past, I can easily show them pictures from the time in question. After all, a picture is worth a thousand words.

The Creative Caveat

I am forever urging people to think in a creative manner. You don't have to toss the photos of your relatives. You just need to know it's okay if you want to! There is one caveat to this "be creative" philosophy of mine: Be practical. One day I was getting a lady settled into her new home. Decision-making was not her strong suit. She wanted to know how everyone else was currently doing something or, better yet, how Martha Stewart did it. On the last day I walked into the kitchen to get a bottle of water and was stopped in my tracks. She had taken all the food out of the pantry and placed her vitamins, alternative medicine remedies, miscellaneous first aid, and suntan lotions on the shelves. It takes a lot to stop me in my tracks, but this bit of creativity did it in spades. I asked her why she had done this and she said, "Well, you've been telling me to come up with creative solutions and I didn't know where else to put these things." Needless to say, food placement was a challenge. Be creative, but don't reinvent the wheel.

Memorabilia

We all save cards, newspaper clippings, and ticket stubs in the belief that these items will be physical reminders of some treasured memory. A problem arises when you have someone who wants to hold on to everything. Even if space is unlimited, you don't need all this stuff cluttering your environment. Consider the lesson of the yellow slicker.

One day a client who is a pack rat was lamenting the fact that some treasured articles of clothing had been discarded. What makes the story remarkable is that Rose was now in her early 60s with two grown daughters. She wished she had saved the yellow slickers they had worn every morning while waiting for the school bus. I asked why these slickers were so memorable. Apparently, they had been worn the year the family lived in Italy. She associated the lost slickers with that special year and the youth of her grown children.

Rose was filled with regrets concerning lots of long-discarded possessions. I came to understand that these articles were like magic talismans in her mind. If she had those slickers, for example, she'd still be young in some way. The past has memories that we legitimately treasure. **If we choose to live in the past, the beauty and potential inherent in this minute in time will escape us forever.**

Remember, too, that you can make scrapbooks from your memorabilia or you can incorporate items into your photo albums. We considered this idea earlier; now let's take another pass at the concept. We've all seen a million wedding albums filled with all the standard shots. Wouldn't it be fun to see a sample invitation in the book? Or perhaps a theatre stub from a London play would perk up your European photo journal. Shadow boxes are wonderfully creative ways to frame precious memorabilia treasures. I've seen a Christening dress with the baby's cap and booties framed, and it was just adorable. I think the real reason most people resist making picture albums and scrapbooks is that they're more often than not done in a boring fashion. We don't know any more about the people when we're done than when we started. Tell everyone a story as you place photos and treasured items on the page. Be aware, too, that a good story follows a natural progression from beginning to end.

Magazines and Catalogues

My rule of thumb about magazines is simple: You don't need more than a year of any one publication. Purchase attractive magazine holders (I prefer the acrylic magazine holders) or use a beautiful basket. When the new issue arrives, toss the oldest issue immediately. Hundreds of magazines tossed into a basket or piled on a table is uninviting and looks sloppy. "Oh! But one day I hope to read those issues!" you lament. May I remind you that the road to hell is paved with good intentions? If you must, peruse the table of contents before you toss the old issue and see if there are any articles you may need for reference purposes.

You can remove the article in one of two ways.

- Keep an article clipper handy.
- Tear the magazine apart by breaking the binding.

If you really do need the article, remember that a Xerox copy lasts longer. In just the same way, replace old catalogues with new ones. Keep them in one tidy spot. Perhaps in that magazine basket near the coffee table? I have an unusually large assortment of catalogues because I do research for clients. I hide my catalogues in the wicker trunk I use as my coffee table and keep them sorted by type. This way if I'm researching a kitchen tool for you, I don't need to rifle through the gardening catalogues or the ones that sell clothing.

The Hall Closet

Pity the poor hall closet. Designed to hold coats and other traveling paraphernalia, it is usually a disaster area. It becomes the official residence for members of the "let's just stick it here" club. Opening the door is a demoralizing experience for family and guests. What belongs in this closet and how do you keep it in order?

- The most commonly used coats of the current season reside here.

- Keep space and hangers for your guests. You'd be surprised how a smooth entry to a home makes people feel genuinely welcome. If you live in a cold climate, be sure and have a few wooden hangers handy to support the weight of the average winter coat.

- Place a shoe rack on the floor to keep the closet tidy. If you live in snow country, a separate boot rack is usually placed by the entry.

- Keep winter hats and scarves in baskets on a shelf so that they do not creep across the shelf, creating a jumble.

- If there is space, put in a second shelf and store some of your out-of-season items here. For example, when it was 95 degrees outside and the humidity was 100 percent back in Brooklyn, I did not want to open the hall closet and be confronted with my winter mittens and scarves.

Keys to the Soul

When I was 13 years old, my mother and I went to the Stratford Theater in Connecticut to see *King Lear*. We stopped at the local pharmacy. Considering how much she liked Shakespeare, my mom was probably looking for tranquilizers or pain relief pills. I was wandering the aisles when suddenly my attention was drawn to a tiny camel. His legs were made of pipe cleaners and his fur was some fuzzy man-made fabric. He was quite unremarkable except for one thing: He had *red* eyes. I said, "Look, Mommy, he has a hangover. We have to take him home!" Today, oh so many years later, over 200 more of his brethren have come to live with me. Some are as small as my finger and one is life-size. I display them with as much panache as I can muster. I have no doubt that some of my guests think this collection is odd. I am almost always asked how it got started. The point is this: The minute you enter my home, you know something very unique about me.

What does your home or office reveal about you? Let's look at some of the things we can use to add a personal touch.

- As suggested, collectibles warm the environment in a unique way. If your collection is extensive, try rotating the pieces for variety and visual interest. By the way, it's very helpful if the physical contents of your home are documented on video or in photographs. In the event of a natural disaster or a theft, this visual record facilitates dealing with your insurance company.

- Pictures reveal your past: where you grew up, what your family members look like, good times you have experienced, and so on. Intentionally reveal aspects of yourself through pictures and creatively display them. For example, I once dated an actor who lined his stairway with still shots from his various movies. It's unique and makes an ordinary trip upstairs an adventure. You could also match the type of photo to the intended activity of the room. For example, I have a client who loves to sail. His library is filled with books on sailing and shipbuilding. He has pictures of his boat and family at play throughout this room.

- Cut flowers add beauty.

- Plants beautify the environment as well as purify the air.

- Lighting is a key element. I have a friend whose family room is so dark it's impossible to read. I cannot count the number of times I have struggled to read a magazine or book while sitting on his couch. Track lighting would solve the problem.

- Fragrance always fills my home whether it's candles or potpourri. I hide scented candles in my clients' closets and place fragrant soaps in their dresser drawers. It's like encountering a little piece of heaven whenever you open a door or drawer to perform some mundane task.

- Finally, let's touch on the use of color. We seem afraid to wear colorful clothes or to experiment with our homes. Be bold! Sponge-paint the guest bathroom purple, stencil cartoon characters on the walls in the baby's room, or paint one red wall in the living room as a dramatic backdrop for a family photo gallery. After all, as long as they continue to manufacture paint rollers, your "mistakes" don't have to be permanent.

The Inanimate Butler

Close to the door you frequently use to exit your house, keep a small table that can hold things you're ready to take out into the world. This might include the sweater that needs to have the wine stain removed or the book you've been meaning to return to the library. Pause here as you exit and ask yourself if you can take care of any of these errands now.

Princess Katie

People have different ideas about house rules for pets. My mother never allowed our collie on any furniture and complained constantly about Queenie's dog hair being everywhere. My Golden Retriever, Katie, rules our home. She sleeps on the couch and next to me on our bed. I make use of covers and wash them weekly. On the other hand, I have clients who have five huge Retrievers and live in a lavishly decorated home. It goes without saying that these animals do not lounge on the couches during the day. The home would be destroyed. You need to find the solution that suits your needs and those of your family members. Strike a compromise and remember it's better to battle with dog hair than have a pristine home without your best friend.

Final Note

Creating comfortable and inviting common rooms isn't about how much money you spend. It's all about how much love and care you invest in the process. If there is discord in your home, strive to heal it as vigorously as you might pour over issues of *Architectural Digest* for design ideas. **It is in the rooms we share with family and friends that being organized gives us an opportunity to nurture the souls of those we love.**

Creativity

CHAPTER 8

Children's Rooms

"Your children are not your children.
They are the sons and daughters of Life's
longing for itself ...
You are the bows from which your children
as living arrows are sent forth ...
... For even as He loves the arrow that flies,
so He loves also the bow that is stable."

—*Kahlil Gibran*, The Prophet

Can you keep a secret? I tucked this very important chapter on children's rooms toward the back of the book for a reason. Your child's room is not the place to start your organizing career. I want your organizing muscle to be strong before you tackle organizing your children.

A Means of Rebellion

Your child will be more inclined to help you create and maintain order in his immediate environment if he is already experiencing its benefits firsthand in the rest of the home. Teenagers tell me all the time that the chaos they live with is mostly a device to drive their parents crazy. I encourage them to find some other way to rebel, as their environment has such a powerful effect on them. Other teens share that they live with chaos because they have no idea *how* to live any differently. This is one of the reasons organizing the common rooms is so important. When a child experiences order in his home, he is more likely to recreate it in his personal environment. If you're a parent who is demanding order in your child's room and the rest of the house looks like a bomb went off, guess what? Your request is meaningless. We teach by example in a more powerful way than mere words can ever hope to convey.

A child's room is a microcosm of every space he will ever have to keep in order. One day it's his room and the next he has moved into a college dorm. Four years zip by and before he knows what happened, he's got his first apartment. Just as you get adjusted to his roommates, he's got a home and family of his own. The cycle of life continues from generation to generation. Assure your children that being organized won't hamper their creativity; it will, in fact, free them to express themselves fully. It will enable them to nurture themselves through their environment. Before you know it, these are the lessons they will be teaching their children.

A Tale of Two Parenting Styles

My wish for you as you begin to work on your child's room is that you will be able to help your child establish a room that is a place where he is allowed to learn about himself and move gracefully into his future. Let me introduce you to two parents who were not able to nurture their children through their environments, even though their love for their children was great.

The first tale is that of my own mother. As I grew into a young woman, my parents generously decided to give me the front parlor on the second floor of our brownstone as my bedroom. Ironically, I was never once asked if I had a vision of any kind for the room. I was not consulted on the furniture that would be purchased. I told my mother that my best friend had my dream room. It was tiny, but the walls were covered with movie posters. I thought it was glorious. "Over my dead body," she said. My mother had a way with words.

After months of construction and shopping, my parents announced the big unveiling was at hand. As I walked up the stairs to the second floor, my fertile imagination pictured all my fantasies waiting for me on the other side of the door ... a huge bulletin board for those coveted movie posters, an enormous bookcase to house my treasured book collection, a fabulous roll-top desk, a mound of stuffed animals on my bed, and, of course, an extra bed for those all-important teen sleepover guests.

My mother was in the new bedroom and, as my father dramatically slid open the pocket doors, she turned on the major light source. I almost had cardiac arrest. The room was lit by a crystal chandelier. There was a four-poster, canopy-top bed, a high boy, a long dresser with a mirror, a desk, a night stand, and a chair. My mother had created the fantasy bedroom *she* had wanted when she was 13. No wonder no one ever asked for my opinion. Ultimately, this room became a vanity display for my parents. Guests were trotted through on the official "after-dinner house tour." I never once slept in that room.

At the opposite end of the spectrum is my client who insists on asking for the opinions of his children at every juncture. One day Hal asked me to accompany them to a furniture store. As a single parent, he wanted a woman's advice. His preteen sons, Josh and Sam, were still sharing a room; however, now they would be able to choose brand-new furnishings. Unfortunately, Josh and Sam could not agree on anything and their father correctly refused to have two different styles of furniture in one small bedroom. Hal felt this was another wonderful opportunity for his sons to learn the value of compromise. Josh and Sam had other ideas. They fought. They wailed. They were intractable. We were in this store for eight hours. I wondered if perhaps I had passed away and this was indeed my personal hell. I finally said to Hal, "Does it have to be their decision? After all, aren't you paying for the furniture?"

Children must be coached in the art of decision-making. The importance of the decisions they make should increase with time and experience. My client got the message and chose his sons' new furniture. It was, by the way, a happy compromise based on what each was drawn to on his own. The difference was that Dad became an active participant.

Stimulating One's Creative Juices

My mother would get a kick out of this chapter. If she couldn't help me pick out furniture, she honored my soul in other ways. It is because of her and not in spite of her that I became a person who nurtures others for a living.

Like all parents, my mother realized she made mistakes. She also recognized and celebrated the things she did well. That's the whole point of this chapter, really. You know by now that I'm not a child psychologist. I'm not even a parent. My job is to help you nurture your children through their environment. Let's take a look at the elements we have to deal with and see what creative solutions we can devise together.

Creating a Personal Haven

Let's start with the basics: furniture! A newborn's furniture is dictated by necessity. The crib, the changing table, the dresser for tiny clothes and diapers, and a rocker for Mom usually fill out the space nicely. As babies grow, their rooms change in proscribed ways. The crib gives way to a first bed. A toy chest and a bookcase make their appearance. Hopefully, the rocker is moved to a corner with a good light source so the child has an inviting space to develop his reading career.

By the time a child is interacting on a regular basis with other children, the room usually morphs into a space that meets the needs of a typical kid. Barbie, GI Joe, and their requisite paraphernalia are soon all in place. We'll discuss ways to keep all of this growing stuff in order. By the time they are teenagers, the desk and computer appear. A TV is very often added. And I, of course, would vote for shelves and at least one file cabinet. I think a child should leave his room with practical organizational skills he can use all of his life.

The Nitty-Gritty

A child's room is going to have all manner of possessions, and keeping it in order can be a challenge. Let's consider a list of things that will help guide our efforts. I've tried to be fairly age-specific in my groups. Some things fall into a gray area and will be applied to a child as his personal maturity warrants.

Baby and Toddler Tips

- Don't buy the store! Be selective when you bring home toys.

- Every six months, spend a few hours weeding out the items that your child has outgrown and/or lost interest in. One of my clients asks her child to literally count the number of gifts he receives for a birthday or holiday. The same number of his old toys or articles of clothing must now be given away. The child gets to choose whether they will be given to some younger child they know personally or to a charity.

- One of my favorite soft animal storage items is a small mesh hammock. It holds a good number of soft toys and keeps them off the floor. It can be quite charming to enter a child's room and see sweet faces floating above the furniture.

   * In a later chapter, we're going to look at the rudiments of Feng Shui, the ancient Chinese art of placement. Since its principles are meant to bring good fortune, don't forget to view the setup of your child's room in accordance with this ancient art. After all, it's never too early to experience good fortune!

The Young Child's Room

   * Keep similar types of things together. In the closet, it will be types of clothing. When it comes to toys, think soft toys/stuffed animals in one container, books and computer games on a shelf, games with pieces (like Legos) in separate containers, and boxed games in another area. Once your child learns this concept, he will use it automatically when he sets up CD and book collections, school and college assignment papers, and so on.

   * Make everything as user-friendly as possible. For example, a toy chest that is a beautiful piece of furniture may be too heavy for little hands to safely open. There are specialty stores that cater to the needs of a child's room. Large chains like Ikea have individual departments devoted to the storage of items a child will be drawn to or need. Catalogue-shop before you leave home in order to develop ideas.

   * Bulletin boards are a wonderful way for a child to keep up with a growing social calendar. Pin invitations here and circle the dates on a calendar. Place pictures of classmates or photos from special adventures. These boards are a good training ground for the daily planners we all carry as adults.

- If you have more than one child, place a large bulletin board in a central location and make a column for each child. I have a client with three children who keeps her board hidden from visitors by hanging it behind a door. She never wants a visiting child to learn of a party he or she has not been invited to attend.

- As your child progresses in school, term papers and special reports become a part of life. Why not give him a small two-drawer filing cabinet and teach him to file school reports the same way we filed your related household papers? Mastering the skill of setting up files will be invaluable later in college and at their place of business. Don't forget that two, two-drawer file cabinets with the flat surface of your choice (glass, wood, or fake marble) placed over them make a really unique and attractive desk. Leave a space for a chair to fit between the file cabinets.

- An organized home reinforces for a child whatever you want him to accomplish in his private quarters. For example, if you have bins in the pantry with snacks, he sees exactly what you are trying to get him to accomplish in his room with his toys or his clothes.

- You want your child's room to grow with him. Don't invest in the most expensive furniture. Children need not be burdened with the responsibility of preserving the finish on their dressers and beds.

- There are heavy plastic containers available now that are on wheels. They make wonderful storage containers for children's toys. In fact, when kids have overnights, a small container on wheels can travel with them.

❧ Where children can play is largely dictated by the size of the home. If the apartment or home is small, it might be helpful to have the children play in their rooms. Having to clean up on a daily basis is a valuable life skill. On the other hand, many parents assign the family room as the place children can spread out their toys and not be responsible for cleaning up until it gets wild and woolly. It's a matter of taste.

Teenagers … Revenge of the Hormones

❧ As children get older, they acquire lots of sports-related equipment. If you have a garage, try and store the items there. It's nice to "fly" bicycles, keeping the floor space clear. A large bin that holds basketballs, footballs, soccer balls, and their related accoutrement is helpful.

❧ Sports shoes take up a lot of room. Wherever you decide to keep them (by the door in the teenager's room, in his closet, in the garage, or in the mud room), do keep them on a shoe rack so that they don't fly all over the room.

❧ Consider a formal, built-in closet system as they get older. It will add to the resale value of your condo or house.

❧ Working with you to decide how much TV and Internet time they can have and still meet their school and family obligations gives your child practice in establishing and maintaining a schedule.

Childhood Memorabilia

After my parents passed away, I moved everything back to New York City. The night before the movers arrived, I made a remarkable discovery. My mother had saved every single notebook I had ever used for the entire eight years I was in grammar school. A friend was helping me and asked, "What are you going to do?" I was overwhelmed. How could I ever sort through eight years of notebooks? I asked my friend to pull out a few and toss the rest.

Lots of parents are exactly like my mom and want to save every drawing, every school notebook, every project. I think it's grand to put drawings on the refrigerator. Be sure to share those reports that were slaved over with every relative who walks through the front door. At the end of the school year, sift through everything and save a few examples of the best your child produced. One day, he's going to inherit this box. If it's a car load of boxes, your son or daughter will be overwhelmed, just like I was on that night I discovered my own childhood treasures.

Opening Night Jitters

Several years ago, I had a featured role in a theater production here in Los Angeles. The character I was portraying was like none I had ever attempted in my career. She was 180 degrees from my own personality. She was insensitive and rude to other people. I understood her pathology, but it hurt me to behave this way. One day, in a panic, with opening night approaching, I called a fellow actor for advice.

Ron is a very kind man who happens to look like your neighborhood rapist or murderer. He is always being cast as a bad guy. I wanted to know how he played those roles without hurting his soul. A pregnant silence followed my question. I've never forgotten what he said. "Well, Regina, first I try and figure out what the writer intended. Then I try and figure out what the director wants." I waited breathlessly. "And then I just try to have fun." Fun? I had forgotten.

Final Note

Being a parent is the most important job you can have. Consider all the things we discussed in this chapter. Weigh the suggestions against the reality of your child and your situation. Do the best you can and then ... have fun! I can reduce the only things I am certain of about children to two sentences: Children live what they are taught. If your child experiences order in his home, he will be more inclined to replicate it in his room. In fact, he'll be likely to pass the skill on to his own children.

和平

Freedom

CHAPTER 9

Physical and Emotional Ties to Chaos

"By a simple breathtaking stroke,
if I can change my mind
and if the world is made
of the same stuff as my mind,
then I can change the world."

—Dr. Deepak Chopra

One of the most nurturing experiences of my professional life was studying acting with Gordon Hunt. In addition to being a gifted director and teacher, Gordon is one of the kindest people I have ever met. After a scene, Gordon would ask the actors to critique their own work. Occasionally, someone would go on and on about the myriad exercises he had done to arrive at an understanding of the character. Gordon told us to be careful about wasting our energy. It is rare, but possible, for a deep understanding of a character to come to you intuitively the minute you read the lines. When it was easy, Gordon would tell us to relax and enjoy the experience.

Tools of the Trade

During the course of reading this book, you may have had an immediate, deep realization about why your past attempts at getting organized have not been as successful as you would have liked. The solution may be as simple as knowing the correct tools to purchase that will solve your space challenge. You may never need or be interested in the information presented in this chapter. *What follows are additional tools for the reader in search of organization in his or her life whose quest may not have been satisfied to date.* I hope those of you who don't need the information will at least enjoy the story.

Coffee Beans 101

As a child not only did I not drink coffee, I could not stand the smell of it. How anyone put that liquid into his or her bodies was beyond my comprehension. My mother compounded matters by dunking her morning toast into this foul-smelling brew. As the butter slick oozed across the surface, I had to leave the table or run the risk of tossing my cookies.

And then I went to college. Coffee enabled me to stay up all night and cram for tests. It perked me up before my late afternoon classes. Coffee kept me warm on cold winter days. I needed it to wake up in the morning no matter what the temperature. Eventually, I perked a pot to help me sleep at night. I thought I had developed a taste for coffee. In reality, I was seriously addicted to caffeine. By the time I moved to California, I was drinking a minimum of 20 cups a day. My skin was gray, my hair limp, I was too skinny, and the only energy I experienced was coffee-induced. Never once did I suspect there was a connection between the vast quantities of caffeine I was consuming and my physical appearance or sense of well-being.

The Teacher Appears

One day the actor who sat next to me in director Gordon Hunt's acting class underwent a dramatic change in his appearance. I had known him for over a year. Week in and week out, he looked like your average guy. Suddenly, his eyes sparkled. He literally glowed with radiant health. His skin was clear. He looked years younger. I had to know his secret. Much to my surprise, he gave all the credit to his doctor. I made an appointment immediately.

Dr. Saram Khalsa is an American-born, Western-trained internist who incorporates Eastern healing modalities into his practice. In the beginning, he was considered an oddball by his peers. Today people fly in from all over the world to see him. His long red beard and his Sikh garb no longer frighten people. He is a renowned diagnostician. In fact, his waiting room has become a gathering place for the rich and famous.

Dr. Saram (all Sikhs who practice the healing arts are "Khalsa") wafted into the room for our first appointment. Imagine my surprise when he announced that coffee was one of several things I had to give up if I wanted to be healthy. "How much coffee do you drink?" he asked. He was apparently willing to let two cups a day slide. When I said my current minimum was 20 cups, his turban seemed to rise about two feet in the air. "And what do you put in this coffee?" he inquired. When he heard artificial sweetener and cream, the nurse had to help me scrape him off the floor.

"Okay," he said gently. "You can't be healthy and drink this much coffee." He asked me to go home and think about my situation. If I wanted to break my addiction, he would help. If I did not wish to alter my consumption, he would not take me as a patient. The choice was mine. No doctor had ever asked me, in effect, to be responsible for my own health. Like most Americans, I thought health could be restored by taking the right pill. This was new territory. I took a month to make my decision.

Ending the Cycle

Breaking an addiction is a challenge. With Dr. Saram's help and visions of Gary's sparkling eyes dancing in my head, I persevered. About six weeks later, my system was caffeine-free. My skin was pink. Friends who saw me in a play at this time told me my eyes sparkled in the stage lights like stars in the sky. I had so much energy I didn't know what to do with myself. It had been worth the struggle and the cost.

I was eager to learn more about creating good health. Dr. Saram continued to be my teacher. When I was sick, he always asked what was going on in my life. He showed me how emotional challenges were reflected in my body. Illness wasn't some evil that attacked me like a demon in a Stephen King novel. It was very often a reflection of a situation I had created or accepted. Not surprisingly, my spiritual teacher at this time was also a pioneer in this philosophy. I was being hammered on all fronts with the concept of self-responsibility.

I'm not suggesting, by the way, that you need to give up coffee. I am suggesting there is a more complicated and delicate relationship between your body and your environment than you may have previously acknowledged. You might be amazed to discover that something outside the immediate realm of getting and staying organized has actually held the key to your failed previous attempts at creating order.

Physical Challenges to Creating Order

Have you ever scheduled a time to get organized only to fall short of your goal? Please take a moment to recall one of those attempts that failed. Now, I'm a very visual person and I can replay events in my mind. If you are not someone who can do this, just think about the experience. Ask yourself these questions:

- Did you wake up too tired that day to tackle the planned task?

- Did you get started and have to stop long before you made any real progress?

- Were you able to push through to completion feeling so worn out you swore getting organized wasn't worth the effort?

- Do you find fatigue gets in the way of most of your scheduled activities?

- Does chronic exhaustion rob your experiences of the fun you anticipated having when they were scheduled?

Instead of feeling defeated because your efforts to get organized were thwarted, why not focus on healing the root cause of the exhaustion that seems to interfere in your plans? I'm addressing a chronic problem. If you can't honor your plan to get organized on Saturday morning because you were given a surprise birthday party the night before, you're a victim of circumstance. If you can't get organized *any* Saturday because you have trouble getting out of bed, you can benefit from addressing the underlying cause of your exhaustion. And what might that be? I'm so glad you asked! Here are just a few of the physical ailments that can get in your way.

Substance Abuse

People take the idea of organizing so seriously, I strive to be as funny as possible when I teach my class. I'm usually assured of a laugh when I announce that it's just about impossible to get organized when you're loaded. A hangover will also put a crimp in your organizing plans. Let's say you're the birthday celebrant at the previously mentioned party. If the celebration was indeed a surprise, why not postpone that organizing project for a day or two?

Attention Deficit Disorder

There are professional organizers who specialize in dealing with people who are challenged by Attention Deficit Disorder (ADD). Concentration is difficult for them. They bore easily. Distractions can be deadly, especially to the ADD-afflicted child. Fortunately, prescription drugs are available to help calm the mental storm. I would investigate natural alternatives and read as many books as I could if I thought this was my challenge. I would caution you to get a professional diagnosis rather than self-proclaim yourself so mentally fragmented by ADD that you'll never be organized. You want to be sure you haven't put a smooth veneer over a much more common problem: laziness.

Peri-Menopause

Ask any woman over 35 for a list of the changes her body is undergoing as she makes the inevitable march to menopause. Near the top, if she is honest, you'll find "an uncontrollable need to nap." I rarely fell asleep on any couch until I turned 40 and I absolutely never slept with makeup on. Suddenly, like some hormone-induced narcoleptic, I could barely pass a couch without at least yawning.

So there you are with a big organizing project on your personal docket and you can barely keep your eyes open. Here are two possible reactions. You club yourself with remorse using a vicious inner dialogue on what a chronic failure you are and how you'll never get organized. Or you join a gym and find a doctor who understands which supplements can help alleviate the situation. I found relief with regular exercise, acupuncture treatments, and Chinese herbs.

In Chinese medicine, they say if you resist the inevitable, you only make matters worse. I have learned to ask my body what it wants and to negotiate with it. I now embrace the concept of naps. I also bought a more comfortable couch. I'd prefer to be 20 again, but since I can't turn back the clock, I accept getting older as a gift not given to every human being.

Epstein-Barr

This virus is also known as chronic fatigue syndrome. You need more than an afternoon nap if this is your problem. You wake up tired and stay exhausted all day. Imagine a person engulfed with physical and mental exhaustion attempting to put together the perfect file system or organizing his or her closets. Ordinary vitamins don't scratch the surface. The lack of energy inevitably leads to depression. Many people find it impossible to continue with their regular schedules. Very often the symptoms are declared to be all in the patient's head and no medical diagnosis is offered.

If I suspected this was my problem, I would find a physician in my area who understood the virus and who could give me the proper guidance. If no physician is available, go to the library and research the health periodicals. Medical doctors are not gods, nor are they all created equal. Sometimes you have to search for the one who understands your illness and suits your personality. Be your own advocate.

And the Beat Goes On ...

It is beyond the scope of this book to list every physical ailment that can tire you into defeat when you set out to tame your environment. Ask questions. Read more. Talk to friends. In the meantime, here are a few more things that can tire the body. I hope this list sparks your investigative juices:

- Hypoglycemia
- Underactive thyroid

&. Diabetes

&. Jet lag

&. Child birth

&. Food allergies

Rock 'n' Roll

When I was a child in Brooklyn, my mother and I used to watch movies on TV together. One that had a powerful effect on me was called *The Rains of Ranchipur*. It was about the destructive force of earthquakes and starred a pre–Elizabeth Taylor Richard Burton. Every time the movie channel decided to run *Rains* for the week, my mother and I would watch it day after day like cinematic junkies. As the earth opened and swallowed actors onscreen, we agreed that living in a place that has earthquakes was crazy. My mother never lived to see me move to Los Angeles.

The Northridge earthquake rocked and rolled everyone who lived through the experience. When the earth stopped moving that morning, my apartment was in shambles. Repairs after a natural disaster take time. A few weeks after the quake, a funny thing happened to me. I looked at my coffee table and saw piles of papers. Nothing you expect from a professional organizer, is it? It actually took me several minutes to realize that night after night I had leafed through these papers like a zombie. I knew what had to be done with each one. I was just too depressed to deal with any of it. **Depression** is an immobilizing force. You can't redo that file cabinet or redesign the way you hang your clothes when you're depressed. And yet you'd be surprised how many people try.

Has something happened in your life to interrupt the normal flow? Have you dealt with it as if it were a separate entity with no effect on all aspects of your life? Let's make a list of some of the triggers for depression:

- Death of a loved one
- Move to a new residence
- Loss of employment
- End of a relationship
- Death of a beloved pet
- Weight gain
- Divorce
- Life-threatening illness
- Natural disasters: fire, flood, earthquakes, blizzards, and so on
- Violent crimes: rape, theft, and so on

The list is endless because we are unique beings who are affected in different ways by diverse forces. The antidotes to depression include the following:

- Exercise, because it releases natural endorphins. There are many kinds of exercise available. At the very least, just put on your coat and go for a walk.

- Perhaps you need to chemically alter your mood to jump-start a return to a normal life? I would consult my doctor and discuss all the choices from Prozac to St. John's wort.

- I am an advocate of therapy with one caveat: Just like physicians, all therapists are not created equal. You need to find one capable of gently holding your hand and guiding you back to stability.

- If no funds are available, try talking to a trusted friend. Very often once the words are spoken, we can begin to experience relief.

* If appropriate, there are innumerable 12-step programs out there. Few things in life are as comforting as a room full of people who share their challenges and who, like us, are making a commitment to mental health.

The Winds of Change

There is a very simple reason some people can't get organized: fear. Unlike the sick-in-the-stomach fear that warns us of imminent danger, this fear is stealthy. Most people affected by it don't realize fear has them in its grasp. They would probably deny it if confronted with the facts. And what is there to be afraid of? Here's a list of "the usual suspects":

* Fear of success
* Fear of failure
* Losing control of one's environment
* Losing control of others

Let's examine these a bit further.

Fears of Success and Failure

These are mirror-image fears. You rarely have one without the other, and, like a set of identical twins, they are often confused for each other. The unconscious pattern at work here warns you that if you get organized, you just might not be able to do what everyone expects of you. Why do you want to face that embarrassment? And if you do succeed by some miracle, even more will be asked, so why bother? What does the human face of this fear look like?

The Open-Door Policy

The work I do with my clients is incredibly intimate. People reveal their secret lives to me. Have you ever seen your best friend's tax returns? Did he ever ask you to refold his underwear? Would you want to sort through the collected memorabilia of a lifetime with him? Chances are I know things about your friend he will not reveal to you. My respect for this level of commitment to change is enormous. I prefer that all such transactions take place in private, but sometimes my hands are tied.

Several years ago I worked with an executive in Northern California. Cheryl is a lovely woman who wanted to be more efficient in her position. She's smart, caring, and willing to learn. We devised simple systems to keep her paper flow in check. We put her physical area in order. We had a wonderful time together except for one thing. The company had an open-door policy and, even though we needed privacy, the door had to remain open.

Beyond the consideration of my client's privacy, I am also sensitive to the emotional life of those with whom they share their work and home environments. We discussed this in the first chapter when we began preparing for our adventure into an organized life. Let's consider for a moment how some of Cheryl's co-workers felt about her endeavors.

It is enormously threatening for most people to watch someone else get organized. It signals a change. The unconscious dialogue runs like this: "If you change, do I have to?" "Will you treat me differently after you're organized?" "Will you advance in stature now that you're in command of your work load?" Obviously, for a person out of touch with his or her feelings, the most expedient thing to do is to sabotage the other person's efforts.

Fear walked into Cheryl's office all day long. Fellow executives came in and offered comments and criticism. I warned Cheryl that the odds were against this type of banter being positive. By the end of the day, she was in tears. Her inner strength prevailed, however, and when I saw her the next day, she was strong and secure about the changes we had made. When you behave in a positive, nonarrogant way like this, you have the opportunity to help others deal with their fears. Your example is the most powerful teacher of all.

Through the Looking Glass

You may identify with Cheryl. Perhaps just recently you tried to get organized and your fellow workers were as frightened as the members of Cheryl's team were. This story may inspire you to continue with your endeavors to have more organization in your life and, in fact, be an inspiration to others. Your desire to succeed is strong and you should be comforted by the work you have done to accomplish this level of support for change within yourself. Cheryl's fear of success came up briefly. It allowed her tears to flow at the end of the day. What an opportunity she had to drop the ball and return to the status quo.

Humans are complex beings. In the workplace, you might find yourself an advocate for change and increased levels of organization. Your home environment may reflect your fears about success. You don't live in a vacuum: The excellent work you do at your place of employment is best supported by a nurturing environment at home. I know a successful mid-level executive whose office is organized as tightly as any branch of the Pentagon, while his home looks like a terrorist group invaded in search of secret documents. He spoke to me at length about his desire to get organized. Every suggestion I had was met with resistance. It took only a few minutes to unearth the hidden agenda: As soon as his home becomes organized, he has promised to marry his long-time sweetheart. As things stood, there was no room for additional paper clips in his home, much less the possessions of another human being.

We bring our fears of success and failure with us like unwanted weights in a backpack. As we march through life, they grow more burdensome. As we confront them, they lose their power over us as quickly as if we tossed the weights from our backpack. It's equally important to remember that there is no right and wrong in these situations. Cheryl might, for instance, have become so unhappy with the treatment she received that the search for a new job would have begun. My male exec might, upon reflection, discover that marriage is the last thing he wants right now.

It's powerful to make life decisions for ourselves. The alternative is to have them made for us by fear. Have you ever seen a small child frightened out of his wits on Halloween because he does not recognize his dad? The sound of that familiar voice emanating from a ghoulish mask doesn't restore confidence. When the mask is removed and Dad says, "Hey, it's me! It's Daddy!" the tears stop. The fear has been literally unmasked. Just so, in our lives we constantly confront fears of success and failure. You can be a champion at work and a wimp at home. A little detective work will make you the all-powerful conqueror, no matter the situation or location.

Final Note

One of my greatest pleasures in life is going to an art museum. From time to time, I have gotten a breath away from some world-famous works of art to study a tiny fragment of the canvas. I try to imagine the artist applying the paint. It is as if the whole story were encapsulated in this tiny blob of paint. If I were to walk into a room at the museum, however, and go from painting to painting looking only at the tiniest of areas on each canvas, I would never understand the pieces. I believe we fragment our lives in this way. And the loss of perspective is just as great. I hope you will now examine your desire to get organized in a new light. You are, after all, like a beautiful canvas, the sum total of all the pieces and not just one exquisite blob of paint.

Growth

CHAPTER 10

Maintenance and Reality

"The power of commitment is available
to transform every unsatisfactory
aspect of our lives
if we are willing to change the assumptions and false
beliefs
that have held us prisoners to our present life
experiences,
while all the time being surrounded by limitless possibilities."

—Noel McInnis

One day, shortly after the first draft of *Zen* had been completed, I looked at my office and realized that it no longer served me. I had been an actress and a businesswoman when I first converted my guestroom to an office. Now I was a writer. *Zen* was in the process of being born and needed special files set up to accommodate the seemingly endless support material. Overnight a crop of new books had appeared and longed for their own bookcase. I needed to embrace a reality that had slowly taken over my life.

A Funny Thing Happened ...

I knew this would be a major undertaking. I would, in effect, be saying farewell to parts of my life. I took a deep breath. I told my Golden Retriever that Mommy was about to make a mess. I crafted a plan on paper and went to the store for supplies. It took three days. When I was done, the room felt different. The visible changes were few. The inner changes in file drawers and the supply closet were extensive. Friends walked in and immediately knew something was different. People intuitively know when an environment has shifted. I told them what I had been up to and they all smiled and predicted that my life was about to change. In truth, it already had. I was just catching up with reality.

Reality: What a Concept!

You can become rich and famous. You can be blessed with servants who cater to your every whim. You can be surrounded by doting family members who do the same. No matter how precious your existence, you are still a human being. You will be buffeted by the winds of change and turmoil in your life. One day you're fine and your home is organized to a point of unimaginable perfection. The next day you wake up and, like me, you realize that your life is different. The change was so gradual and natural, you missed the moment your new life and your old environment stopped working in concert. At other times, there may be a sudden and dramatic disruption in your life. Without warning, your spouse wakes up with the flu and needs special attention. Used tissues fly about the floor, dispersing germs to other members of the family. Suddenly, all the kids are wheezing and achy as well. Everyone needs your attention. Lo and behold, even Fido begins to sneeze! Being organized means you are in a powerful position when it comes to dealing with life's unexpected changes.

The Real Deal

Getting organized is a creative, vibrant, ongoing endeavor. Are you the family member who slaves over a hot stove on

Thanksgiving Day? You could shellac the food into an artistic still life and never have to cook the meal again. It's just that eating on the holiday would require a new solution. Have you dusted lately? We all know it will have to be done again. Did you enjoy your last breakfast? Tomorrow morning your body will expect another meal. We live in a world that requires maintenance.

The Good News

Once you create the systems you are comfortable with, they remain in place waiting to be restored. Remember the spouse who had the flu and needed you to wait on him hand and foot? The mail piled up on your desk. Two weeks went by and your home office looked like a bomb went off. Guess what? All you need to do is schedule some time to put everything in its place. You don't have to re-create the system *every* time you encounter a little chaos.

The other day a client lamented that she had trouble finding the time to work on her home office. I decided to go out on a limb and give her my honest opinion. If you have healthy self-love and high self-esteem, you will make the time because you honor yourself as a human being and respect the work you feel called to accomplish. You'll want to work in peace and calm. No schedule, no relationship, no hardship, no obstacle of any kind can stand in the way of this kind of resolve. In fact, the only thing that ever comes close to standing in my way is that long-suffering look my Golden Retriever gives me when I launch into a big project that threatens to overtake her territory. A long afternoon romp in the park is the accepted bribe!

The Wisdom of Edna

A few years ago, an 85-year-old lady decided to take my class. Edna told me while she still had her health, she wanted to put her affairs in order. She wanted to make things as easy as possible for her children when she made her transition. Like many women from her generation, no one had ever taught Edna how to set up files or keep records. Ironically, my next class was equally divided between homemakers and corporate executives. I hoped Edna wouldn't feel intimidated or lost.

I called her a week after class to see how she had enjoyed the material. I wanted to be sure she felt her needs had been met. She told me she had been fascinated rather than intimidated by the businesspeople. Edna promised she would keep me posted on her progress. Six months passed without a word from her. One day I received a beautiful letter telling me that her organizing work had sent her on a personal journey of discovery. She had indeed put her affairs in order. She had sorted through the treasures of a lifetime. It had been slow going, but she was determined. Nothing could deter her from the work she had set out to accomplish.

Like Edna, every day we are asked to make decisions. We make plans. We schedule social events and work assignments. Choices rear their sweet little heads and we are unconsciously asked to renew our resolve. Practice really does make it easier. The last I heard, by the way, Edna was encouraging her friends to get organized. Knowing Edna, she's probably devoting her free time to learning a new sport! She traded the time she was spending worrying about the state of her affairs for free time she could devote to the process of living in the moment.

Modus Operandi

Maintenance is an ongoing task. The majority of my clients work outside the home and have housekeepers and assistants. Lacking the funds to have this level of help, you can do several simple things each day to help maintain a feeling of peace and calm. The short list of things to do before you leave your house for work (even if that means going down the hall to your home office) includes the following:

- ❧ Making your bed every morning
- ❧ Never leaving dirty dishes in the sink
- ❧ Putting the clean dishes away
- ❧ Never leaving untidy stacks of papers, magazines, or newspapers on the coffee table, the night stand, or anywhere else for that matter

The good mood from a productive day will instantly begin to erode when you are confronted with the chaos of an unmade bed, dirty dishes stacked in the sink, clean ones piled high in the dish rack, or mountains of unread periodicals and untended papers. Make a conscious investment of time to alter your habits when it comes to maintaining your environment.

Remember what we observed about the creation of a new habit? It takes 21 consecutive days before a new task becomes ingrained as a habit. Why not make acquiring this new habit a game? Getting organized doesn't have to be a homework assignment.

Here's an exercise to help you focus your energy:

1. Take out your daily planner. Pick the day on which you want to start making the bed before you leave the house. (I would suggest tomorrow.)

2. Place the number 1 in red ink on the chosen date and circle it in red.

3. On the twenty-first day, schedule a treat as a reward. Write it on your calendar. Do it in red as well. Make it something that's good for you like a movie with your best friend or the first manicure you've treated yourself to in years. You get the idea here. The reward has to be something that helps motivate you to get to the finish line.

If you get sabotaged midstream, follow the guidelines we employed at the beginning of this book. Examine exactly what happened that derailed your good intentions:

* Did you get distracted?

* Was someone else the culprit?

* Are you confronting simple, psychological avoidance or is life sending you a curve ball? It's important to be able to differentiate between laziness, for example, and the needs of a very sick child as you start your day.

Whatever caused the blip in your progress, take a deep breath and start over again. You may not believe this, but the day is just around the corner when one dirty dish will bother you if it's left in the sink. You will not be able to leave the house knowing a rumpled bed is waiting to greet you when you return home. It's not about doing any of these things because your mother or your spouse thinks you should or because you read it in this book. You make these changes because you love and respect yourself.

The Winds of Change

Incorporating new habit patterns is a challenge I rather like. In fact, I love change when I am its architect. When it overtakes me and overhauls key areas of my life, it is, as they say, a horse of a different color. As the end of this book appeared on the horizon, a profound change in the everyday landscape of my life occurred. I want to tell you about my experience and connect what I ultimately learned in this world of organization that I have been sharing with you. And you thought making the bed was a chore!

The Story of Susie

The phrase "best friend" has become a cliché. People seem to use it to describe even the most casual of friends. Let me introduce Susie by saying she is the person who taught me the meaning of the word *friend*. Susie is always there for me whether I needed a shoulder to cry on or a companion for the movies. Ten years into our friendship, she became my business mentor. The landscape of my life would have been barren without the presence of this wonderful, giving, caring human being.

Prince Charming ... Delayed

As her fortieth birthday loomed on the horizon, Susie made a startling announcement ... "Prince Charming doesn't appear to be coming," she said, "and so I'm going to adopt a baby." Susie's plans evolved over time. The next announcement was her intention to journey to Russia to adopt a little girl. On the video snippets chosen by the adoption agency, the baby looked like an angel. Even I was smitten. Susie flew to Russia, took the 14-hour train ride to the town where the orphanage was located, and returned to Los Angeles with the baby whose new name was Molly. She more than lived up to her video introduction.

I had feared the presence of a baby would so change Susie's life that our friendship would suffer. Over the years, I watched as women friends became "Super Moms," leaving friends and sometimes even spouses in the wake of their devotion. Happily, Molly did not cause a rift between us; she joined the friendship. In fact, Molly could not be more like Susie if she had indeed been carried in her womb. It has been a blessing for all of us who know and love Susie to share the joy of loving Molly.

Tidal Wave

Susie had become the desktop publisher of my *Zen* manuscript. I was two chapters from completion when she dropped
a bomb: She and Molly were moving to Phoenix. Susie's family had moved there several years ago. She felt it was a safer,
saner place to raise Molly. Intellectually, I agreed.

Emotionally, I was devastated. For 20 years, Susie had
never been more than three miles from my front door. Now
she would be in another state. As moving day drew closer,
friends called, faxed, and e-mailed their condolences to me. I
refused to deal with my feelings. I said inane things like the
move would give me an opportunity to visit the Grand
Canyon. People stared strangely at me. Thank goodness, no
one laughed.

Susie's new company offered her a moving package. I was
hired to supervise the move and do the unpack. Turning an
empty house into a home is my specialty. About a week before
the move, I stopped at Susie's to do some editing on her computer. Just inside the front door, she had a photo gallery. It had
been packed. The sight of those boxes and that bare wall made
me sick to my stomach. At that moment, the reality of losing
my best friend hit me.

I realized I could turn the Phoenix house into a home, but
I could not participate in tearing the current one apart. Putting
things in boxes was the physical, unavoidable signal that the
move was a reality. Later Susie told me she experienced the
same emotional reaction to the sight of the disappearing possessions and the manifested boxes. Our solution was to employ
my wonderful assistant to supervise the movers on packing day
and the cleaning crew the day after, and to work with Susie the
last hours she was in residence in Los Angeles.

This move reminded me of the importance of recognizing the emotional component of the tasks we must perform in life. Here I was, a professional organizer, stopped in my tracks by my emotions. How much more debilitating would this move have been had I not had my skills to draw upon? My assistant told me to write about this move in my book. I hope it illustrates for you in a graphic and personal way how important it is to honor your feelings and, perhaps most important, to reach out for help when you need it.

As of this writing, by the way, Susie and Molly are settled in their new home. We're already able to laugh about the sorry state of our health during the unpack. We were both poster children for bronchitis! About a week after my return, Susie called to pay me the highest compliment. She was able to find everything because it was all put away in the most logical places available in the house. The principles taught here will assist you in creating order no matter how difficult the situation.

A Moving Experience

Few things in life are as disruptive as a move. The key to a successful move is preparation. Whether you are one of those people who moves every few months or someone who hasn't changed residences in a long time, this book will serve you well.

Let's take a look at some of the steps you'll need to take to ensure a successful move. Remember that an organized household is much easier to transport. If you haven't had an opportunity to put your home in order, moving is a wonderful incentive. You may be forced to downsize because the new locale is smaller. Or you may find yourself thinking of rearranging the furniture to accommodate the new layout. No matter what work lies ahead, this book will guide you to a sane transfer of possessions.

Phase One: Finding the Movers

- Even if you have the 12 original apostles handle the move, something is bound to break. It pays to hire experienced, professional movers to pack for you and purchase their insurance. Reputable movers have repair people they can send your broken items to for restoration. Should they be destroyed, you will at least be reimbursed. The key here is to realize that human beings are moving you and sometimes human beings make mistakes. If nothing gets broken or damaged in any way, you will have the luxury of being pleasantly surprised.

- If you do all of the packing yourself, you may indeed save a few dollars. Consider, however, how exhausted you are going to be. How long will it take you to recover your strength and be able to enjoy the new digs? Pay the movers to pack your home. They will do it better and faster than you can.

  On the other hand, professional movers are not the people to do your unpacking. If one is available, you'll want to employ a professional organizer. Movers literally unpack you, leaving a sea of possessions scattered about the home or office. They do not put things away nor do they organize.

- Research your moving company carefully. Have they been used by friends? Are there any complaints lodged against them at the Better Business Bureau? Do they hire extra help on an as-needed basis or is there a set crew? What is the relationship between the employee sent to your home for the estimate and the crew that will do the actual move?

❧ Provide lunch and sodas for your movers. If you appreciate the work they have done, give them a tip at day's end.

❧ By the way, most moving companies will require cash or a cashier's check. One day a surgeon client handed me a personal check for the movers. I presumed he had cleared this as the accepted manner of payment. The next day the movers would not unload the truck until a certified check appeared. The good doctor was hauled out of surgery. Need I say more?

❧ When the rep from the company comes to view your possessions and give you an estimate, ask for all available literature. This material is always invaluable for the person who does not move very often as it delineates what steps need to be taken and provides a timeline.

❧ For moves requiring that your possessions travel a long distance or be kept on the truck for several days, be sure and ask your mover about putting artwork in crates. Be sure they are experienced in moving high-end items. The same is true for moving a piano. If the movers aren't experienced at moving pianos, there are specialty companies who will see that it arrives safe and sound.

Phase Two: Advance Planning

❧ You'll need to call your utilities and establish a cut-off date and a turn-on date at the new location. Interstate moves are more complicated as you'll need to open new accounts. Allow plenty of time for credit checks and transfer of funds. Open a local bank account as soon as possible.

- ❀ Get change of address forms at the post office. Remember to advise your family, friends, co-workers, magazine subscriptions, charities, etc. of the impending move. It can take up to two weeks for the transfer of mail to become effective. Ask your mail carrier when he would advise you to let the post office know about your plans. Give the world at large at least two weeks to adjust their records. For the computer literate, e-mail is a marvelously quick way to let the world in on the upcoming change. During the transition, people will still be able to communicate with you.

- ❀ Reorder stationery as soon as you know all the new information.

- ❀ If you're moving to a condo, find out ahead of time if there are any restrictions about hanging things on the walls or placing furniture and plants on the balconies or terraces.

- ❀ If you have an expensive art collection, secure the services of a company that specializes in hanging artwork.

- ❀ Surf the Net to get as much information about the new area as possible. Knowing the local parks, recreation centers, department stores, and so on can be especially helpful for those members of the family who are making the move under duress. The Net will also provide driving directions. You can get routes from your house to the local market, bank, and so on before you arrive.

- ❀ Ask your realtor for information about the school district in your new neighborhood. Surf the Net for your children's interests. It may help if you can share specific information with your children about the new area. We all need something to look forward to when life is asking us to say good-bye.

🐾 Your pets need special care during a move. It can be a time of tremendous emotional upset for them. In the last chapter, we'll deal with this in more detail.

Phase Three: Getting Ready for the Big Day

Don't take everything to the new location with the assumption that some day you'll sort through the possessions of a lifetime. Employ our three-step formula to organize the house before the movers arrive. If you have had a chance to use this book and your house is already in order, most of the work is done. If you have not had an opportunity to organize your home, this will be a wonderful opportunity for a fresh start. Here's how it will work:

🐾 **Eliminate** what you no longer need, whether this means trashing, donating, or giving the items in question to someone else. This is especially important on interstate moves because your moving van will stop at a weigh station. You'll not only be hauling things with you that you don't need, you'll now be paying for the privilege!

🐾 **Categorize** items so that they will be easier to pack. For example, if you have tools in the kitchen that should have gone into the garage years ago, place them there so that they will arrive in the appropriate location in the new house. Are there items in the attic you want to store in the new garage? Move them there now. You get the idea.

🐾 **Organize** the actual move in a way that will help the movers and save time. If you can eliminate half of the "Where does this go?" questions, you'll not only be saving time, but money as well. The person who writes up the estimate is sometimes the driver of the moving truck. He will supervise the worker bees the day of the move. More often than not, however, the person who gives the estimate does that for a living. He will write all of your special requests down. The worker bees are the engine that drives the move. They rarely stop to assimilate those detailed instructions. All day long you'll be asked questions unless you prepare ahead of time. How does this work? Grab a pencil and some paper. Later you can three-hole-punch these sheets and turn these notes into your official moving notebook.

1. On the first piece of paper, list all of the rooms in your current residence. Now, take a minute to list all the rooms in your new home. You'll notice that some rooms are the same. For example, your kitchen boxes should be labeled "kitchen" and there is only one logical place for them in the new home. Note all the rooms that keep the same names. If any furniture is to be put in a new place, tag it with the appropriate destination. (You can use garage sale tags and tie them on to handles. They are available at all stationery and office supply stores.)

2. The confusion sets in when you have a room you currently refer to in one way, such as "the den," and in the new home that den furniture is going into a room to be known as the "downstairs guest bedroom." The bigger the homes, the more probability of confusion. Be sure you can identify the correct destination of a room's contents. If your movers take things up and down stairs unnecessarily, they won't be happy. You want happy movers.

3. If you don't tell the movers how you refer to each room, they will come up with their own names. A room you now regard as a den may appear to be a family room to the movers. You can drive yourself crazy on moving day trying to decode the names the movers have assigned to your rooms. Or worse, you can be at a nice hotel and your professional organizer will be driven nuts! Large typed or computer-generated notes in each room will help the movers. At the entry to a room, I tack up an instruction sheet for the movers. For instance, in the kitchen, my note would say something like this: Mover Alert: Please pack all contents of this room and label the boxes "Kitchen."

4. I use dots in rooms that will have an identity change. In the den of our example, I might write something like this: Mover Alert: Please place red dots on all the boxes coming out of this room and label the boxes "Downstairs Guest Bedroom." At the new house, I'd tack up a red dot outside the door to this room and tell the movers to remember that all boxes with red dots go here.

Going Dottie

A word of caution about using dots. I explained this technique to an elderly lady over the phone. "Dottie," as I like to call her, was living back East and planning a move to Los Angeles. She said she understood how to use the dot technique. When her belongings arrived in California, the movers and I were a bit confused. The boxes were *covered* with dots, as were the individual contents. When she arrived several days later, she explained that there were four colors of dots. Each dot signified a location. In this example, there were multiple locations for the contents of the original dwelling. Here's the problem. You must tell the people in charge what the colored dots mean. You cannot put items for multiple locations in one box. Colored dots need to indicate one destination and someone at the new location should know the meaning of the dots.

Phase Four: Preparing the New Location

- You want the new location to be ready for your arrival. Be sure the necessary repairs, any painting, and cleaning are completed before the moving truck arrives. If the closets or the garage need additional storage added, have that work done as well. I encourage clients not to tackle any major remodeling for at least six months, especially if they are newlyweds. I also urge clients to double the time any contractor gives them as the target for job completion. Expecting delays will keep you sane. If none come up, you'll be pleasantly surprised.

- Set aside a bathroom for the movers. Be sure and have soap, toilet paper, and paper towels available.

- Work out a game plan for unpacking, especially if you do not have a professional organizer. Here are some of the details you need to consider:

  1. Decide what you'll want to unpack first (ask the movers to load those items last so that they are the first to come off the truck). By the way, wardrobe boxes are expensive. You'll want to unpack them first so that the movers can take them and not charge you. It's very important they be loaded last; otherwise, you won't stand a ghost of a chance trying to unpack them quickly. Be sure the cartons aren't

overloaded. I've seen moves where the clothes are so wrinkled, nothing can be worn without being washed and pressed or sent to the cleaners. You need one person to supervise the movers and one to start unpacking these boxes immediately.

2. Project how many days you will allot for unpacking. Set daily goals.

3. Line up assistance if no organizer is available. Be sure your helpers understand their role is to assist you and not to make decisions for you. In other words, don't ask your mother-in-law to come over until you're settled.

4. Arrange for childcare, especially if you have young children. The pandemonium of a move can be very unsettling for small children. They will react more favorably to the move after their new rooms are set up. You need to be free to supervise the movers, not the children.

5. Have you made travel provisions for the animals in your household? Dogs tend to be very adaptable, needing only the presence of their owners to feel safe and secure. Cats require special care. Why not speak to your vet and get some professional tips on making the transfer a pleasant one. In any case, be sure Fido and Kitty have fresh water at all times.

6. If you are purchasing a house, remind the former owners to leave the warranties and instruction booklets for all major appliances. Remember to do the same for those who have purchased your home. Garage door openers and extra keys are important things to collect and/or leave behind.

On the Road Again

Most of my clients go to a hotel the first two days after the move. This gives me a chance to work around the clock converting the new house into a home. A hotel stay involves that time-honored tradition: packing a suitcase. Since most people take everything but the kitchen sink with them no matter how short the visit, I thought it would be wise to offer a few timely tips about the art of packing. When you read the last chapter of the book, you'll find tips for business and pleasure packing.

Final Note

Keeping an organized home allows us to be more mobile. Getting this home organized, however, isn't just a five-hour task for a Saturday afternoon. It is part of the very fabric of your lives. Don't think of this as work or a burden. Make your daily organizing rituals and your special projects sacred tasks. One of the most sacred tasks of our lives is establishing a home. It is, after all, the physical dwelling place for our souls and all the beings God has given to our care.

Chi

CHAPTER 11

Benediction

"When it [worship] comes from your heart,
it goes beyond all the known universe,
beyond the most distant of galaxies,
and reveals the sweetest truth of all—
the Creator of all this is our
own Divine Companion."

—*Ramakrishna*

Once your environment is systematized and full of peace, you may want to have it blessed. You can do this yourself by simply standing in the middle of your living room, filled with love for your environment, and exclaim, "God bless this home!" You may also want to explore the way other cultures and religious groups have gone about this ancient practice.

Creating Sacred Space

Let's look at some examples of creating sacred space that other religions have offered their practitioners. When I was a Catholic, for example, a priest was invited to our Brooklyn home one night for dinner. Before he left, my mother asked him to give the house a blessing. It wasn't because of any bad feelings or for any special occasion, it was just a sign of her love for our home. After my parents passed away, their retirement home developed an odd feeling that made me uncomfortable. I called a priest friend and asked him to give a blessing that would dispel any negativity that had settled over the house.

Jews often place a mezuzah at the entrance to the home to protect it from evil. The son of dear friends just had his Bar Mitzvah. He is, like his father, an extremely gifted musician. Knowing that he will be going off to college in a few years, I gave him a mezuzah with piano keys on it to take with him. I hope it protects him as he prepares to be an independent man in the world. I also hope it makes him smile whenever he looks at it. Christians frequently put pictures of Jesus or the cross in their homes. I'm sure rabbis, priests, and ministers of all faiths have a multitude of blessing practices they can share with members of their congregations.

Many Paths, Many Blessings

The Native American culture is rich with ways to clear the space and make it sacred. Following this tradition, lots of people now routinely wave a burning sage stick to clear a space of old energy patterns. Yogis clear a space by waving a stick of burning incense around the frames of the doors and windows to protect and clear the entrances to the home. This is accompanied by the proscribed ringing of a small bell and specific prayers. The Chinese culture might employ various Feng Shui techniques (pronounced *fung shway*). If you choose to clear and bless your home, you have to investigate only the avenue that makes you most comfortable. For me, the path to the sacred was found in the Chinese practice called Feng Shui.

Demystifying Chi

Chi is the Chinese word for *energy*. As Westerners, we tend to have a concept of energy based solely on how we feel. "I just don't have the energy to ..." or "Where do you get all your energy?" I realize, therefore, that for many of you discussing energy strikes you as a bit odd. Long before I ever dreamed I would understand this concept, I had two visceral introductions to the world of energy. The first was a powerful demonstration of the presence of evil. When I was 18, my parents generously sent me on a two-month tour of Europe. While we were in Germany, I decided to visit Dachau. I could not have explained at that tender age that the palpable heaviness in the air was due to the catastrophic acts of violence committed in this spot. Now it seems obvious. Many years later, when I met the brilliant Dr. Linda Zhang, she introduced me to Chinese medicine. Dr. Zhang was kind enough not only to treat me as a doctor, but to take the time to teach me the underlying concepts behind acupuncture. As you probably know, acupuncture involves putting needles into the body. Energy meridians flow in the body. When the chi becomes blocked, you have stagnation of the natural energy flow. This stagnation is the underlying cause of our physical ailments. Correct placement of a needle allows the chi to begin flowing correctly again. The needles are, by the way, much thinner than a standard American needle and are not painful. One might say that Feng Shui is acupuncture of the physical space.

The Ancient Art of Placement

What exactly is Feng Shui and how can it help you? It is called "the art of placement," and there are two schools of thought. One is the compass school, and its understanding of the flow of chi in a space is taken literally from the compass. The other is the Black Hat Sect, founded by Professor Lin. I have studied the latter and I will share its basic precepts with you here. Please keep in mind that it takes years of study to understand and master this ancient art. Here you are being given just a few humble hors d'oeuvres from the vast Feng Shui platter!

Practitioners of each path tend to be very devoted to its teachings. Which should you study? Is one "better" than the other? Allow me to share my Guru's wise counsel about finding your true spiritual home. Study all paths. Go to services at churches, temples, and synagogues. One day you will know that you are "home." When that happens, devote yourself to your path. The feeling of being at home is a reflection of the joy your soul feels as you set foot in the direction you were born to walk.

It is wonderful advice to heed as you explore the many facets of Feng Shui. The intuitive school appeals to me because you can practice it in any location. You do not need to concern yourself with specific directions. The examination of the room will follow from standing in its main entrance and using the bagua. Now, I have gotten ahead of myself. Let's return to our study of chi.

In Chinese philosophy, *everything* is made of chi. This energy is the life force operating in the world. When a home or office is built, the chi is enclosed in an area. An eight-sided diagram called the bagua is used to distinguish the parts of the home that govern various aspects of our lives, such as relationships, prosperity, creativity, and so on. You mentally place the diagram over the house as a whole and then again in each room. Bagua, by the way, as exotic sounding as it is, simply means "eight" in Chinese.

The Bagua

Let's look at this diagram and learn the meaning of each part of the room.

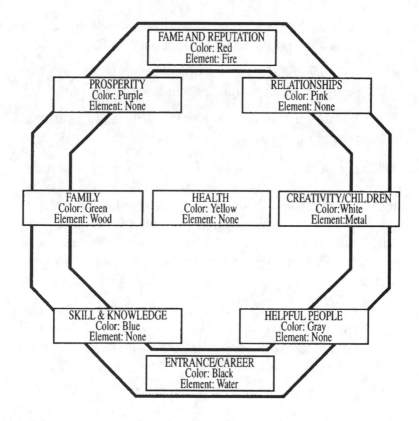

As you see, a quality of life (prosperity, relationships, wealth, and so on), a color (purple, pink, green, and so on), and, in some cases, an element (fire, silver, and so on) are indicated for each area. Consider the prosperity corner. You don't have to have a purple corner painted into every room of your house. People will wonder about your fashion sense. The color purple can be visible in a candle or a decorative item or be prominent in a painting. It can also be hidden. Trace the bagua shape in purple construction paper and place it behind a painting or under a table. As you do so, you should do three things:

1. Place the bagua with intention (understand why you are using a purple bagua in lieu of a pink one).

2. Visualize the changes in your life that increased prosperity (or whatever quality is indicated) will bring.

3. Release this vision with a prayer tailored to your conception of communication with God.

Following the diagram, you can bless every room of your home or your office. When my clients want to have an official blessing, I ask them to call my teacher, Feng Shui master Nate Batoon. If, on the other hand, they simply wish to have some Feng Shui tips, I am happy to share my knowledge with them. Here are some of the most common tips I share with my clients:

- Try not to set up a room so that your back is to the door. This is a weak position. Turn your desk or chair so that you are able to see everyone as they enter and leave your space.

- Do not position your bed at home or your chair at work so that you are in line with the door. This is especially true in offices that enforce the open-door policy. Feng Shui says you will be weakened by the energy traveling down that hall toward you in the person of every human being walking that path.

- When you are away at work, your pets are wonderful ambassadors of Feng Shui. Your dogs and cats keep the chi from becoming stagnant in your absence. Doesn't that make up for the fact that Fido isn't a tax-deductible expense?

- Table-top fountains are all the rage now and, if placed in the entrance (to the building or in an office), invite prosperity. Water represents money and the movement of the water suggests the flow of wealth into your life. Ever wonder why Chinese restaurants traditionally have a fish tank? And you thought it was a love of fish!

❧ Plants build the chi in a space.

Feng Shui Cures

I can just hear some of you screaming, "But … but … I can't do those things! My desk is stationary in my cubicle!" or "I can't stand the sound of running water! Does this mean I can't be prosperous?" The great thing about Feng Shui is that there is always a cure for what ails the space. Let's see how we can alter our list to suit individual needs:

❧ Can't move the desk? Place a mirror at eye level so you can see whoever enters the space. Try and find an eight-sided mirror to add a little power in the mix.

❧ No other way to configure the rooms where you sleep or sit?

  ❧ In Feng Shui the belief is that, where there is an obstruction, a plant will help the chi flow more harmoniously. I would place a blanket chest at the foot of the bed and put a beautiful plant on top of the chest.

  ❧ I had a long organizing assignment once and the office I was given to use was a Feng Shui nightmare. The desk sat between *two* doorways for starters. In this instance, there was a resident plant person, so I asked for a large fern to be placed in front of my desk and removed one of the chairs. I wasn't a permanent executive and the likelihood of two people coming to sit and chat were remote. I also employed another powerful Feng Shui cure.

✤ I hid two five-inch bagua mirrors: One faced the front door and was taped to the modesty panel of the desk. The other mirror was hidden in the file drawer and faced my client's office. Mirrors reflect back whatever is being sent to you. I have one taped to the front door of my apartment as I type these words. Knock on my door with a heart of love and love is reflected back to you. Come to me with anger in your heart and I return the favor without saying a word.

✤ If you hate pets, don't get any! Be aware, however, they do make small fish bowls with swimming artificial fish.

✤ Are you bothered by the sound of running water from a fountain? Find yourself running to the bathroom more frequently? Use something else that represents water like a fish rug or sculpture. Make sure the fish faces inside so that you are asking that increased funds flow into your pockets, not out the door!

✤ Kill every plant you gaze at? A silk plant will do the job. Be sure and add a tablespoon of soil. I tell my clients to bring soil from a place they love like a garden they enjoy.

Feng Shui Detective

I loved my old Mercedes and nursed her along to the bitter end. One day I was waiting at my auto mechanic's for his diagnosis. As I sat there, I began to idly study his office from a Feng Shui perspective. I knew him to be a pretty open guy, so after he told me about my car, I asked if he wanted to know what Feng Shui revealed about his space. He said yes and here is the gist of what I told him.

* He was consistently very creative about finding ways to bring money into the business, but it tended to flow right out the door.

* He had lots of skilled workmen, but they didn't seem particularly interested in furthering their knowledge. In addition, they didn't stay with him for years as he would have preferred.

* Although his business was an established one, he had trouble getting people to be aware of him.

* His existing clients were very loyal to him.

My poor mechanic turned ghostly white. He told me I was exactly right on every count. What had told me all of this, he wondered? Here are the things I observed:

* The "creativity wall" was full of beautifully framed cars. These images were actually in every available space of the office. Anyone who loved beautiful cars would be inspired in this office.

* The "prosperity" corner was a bathroom (symbolizing drainage of money).

* "Fame and reputation" was a second doorway to the outside world. Ironically, it was a small space and it seemed that the money coming in had a literal physical door to fly out of.

* "Skill and knowledge" was barren. There was a small window in this corner that looked into a tiny storage room. This room was in chaos.

* "Helpful people" was occupied by his devoted cousin's desk and the file cabinets holding all client records.

I told him about some Feng Shui cures and he promised to implement them in time. I lost touch with my old mechanic when I changed vehicles, but will always remember two things about him: his openness to another culture's teachings and his willingness to try the suggested changes. Are you curious about the Feng Shui cures I suggested? Here they are:

- To stop the flow of money outside the business, I suggested he wrap a nine-inch strip of red electrical tape around the pipes in the bathroom. This is an ancient cure whose origins are lost. I can tell you that red is an activating color in Feng Shui and that nine is considered the most powerful number.

- The prosperity corner could be energized by hanging a chime.

- The color of prosperity is purple, so it wouldn't be expensive or difficult to use purple hand towels in the bathroom.

- The family area was barren except for a run-down, uncomfortable, old chair. I suggested he purchase a new futon couch as a way of inviting customers to actually sit down while symbolically communicating to his employees that he wanted them to feel welcome as well. The family area represents familial relationships with everyone in your life.

- A small, decorative water fountain on a black metal stand placed in the entrance would help activate business. It would also be very soothing to my mechanic and his cousin as they tended to paperwork and phone calls. Needless to say, Mercedes repairs can be costly so the clients would be soothed as well.

❧ As you enter a space, you are facing the Fame and Reputation area. I asked them to place a picture of a red sports car here. It would serve as a conversation piece, pick up people's spirits as they entered, and energetically promote the business in the world.

No matter how mundane your business is, you want to draw employees and customers into an atmosphere of warmth and caring. You can accomplish this in many ways. Candy, for instance, on a reception desk is a very welcoming, inexpensive (dare I say it?), sweet touch. Flowers and plants warm up the coldest environment. Here we could not use anything alive because there were chemical fumes. Silk arrangements were suggested to promote the same warm response. Do you remember the office that was a Feng Shui nightmare? I kept candy on my desk at all times and I hid potpourri in the room. Whenever people came to visit, they felt very welcome. Food and scent are primal.

Feng Shui as Teacher

Throughout this book, I have periodically asked you to do a written exercise. I'm sure the others felt a lot like homework from your school days. I want you to shift now into play mode. Grab a few sheets of paper and your favorite writing instrument. Take your supplies, grab your beverage of choice, and settle down in your favorite room of the house. Ready?

1. Please draw a square on an 8½ by 11-inch sheet of white paper. Write the name of the room over the square so you know where you are. Later you may want to apply this exercise to every room in your home and to the home itself.

2. In the square, either sketch in the furniture or write the names of the furniture pieces in the appropriate place. I can't draw to save myself, so I'd write in the words couch or hutch and mark with an X.

3. Copy the following list and write it next to your square:

   ❧ Entrance

   ❧ Near-left corner

   ❧ Far-left corner

   ❧ Left wall connecting the above corners

   ❧ Wall straight across from the entrance

   ❧ Far-right corner

   ❧ Near-right corner

   ❧ Right wall connecting the above corners

   ❧ The center of the room

You have already noted the furniture, so what I want you to be aware of now are all the extraneous things like newspapers or magazines, dying plants, dirty laundry, or a cat litter box that may be occupying your space. Note what is in each area and write "nothing" if it's clear. If an area has no furniture but you placed something special on the wall, like a family photo gallery, please make note of that. Did you unconsciously place your photos in the family section? Just for fun, also write down the predominant color in each area. For example, one of my clients has the most beautiful purple velvet sofa. The color is exquisite and attention getting. You'd be remiss if you didn't note the color.

Piles 'O Things

Organizing your home eliminates piles of things. *Piles inhibit the flow of chi.* What's the condition of the far-left corner of the room you chose? What is there now? Is it cluttered with piles of unread magazines? Have you placed a garbage can there? One client had her cat's litter box strategically placed in this corner. This is the prosperity corner of any room. I asked her to look at her finances and see if money flowed freely into her life. Removing those pesky piles might just free up your flow of money. Look at the bagua and see what areas of life each part of the room governs. If an area is piled high with stuff, ask yourself how healthy the part of your life represented by that area is. Are you in quest of a relationship? What's in that corner of your favorite room? One of my clients was trying to repair his marriage. His home was lovely and clutter-free. During one visit, by chance, I saw what was behind his garage, the far-right hand corner of his lot. Here, in the relationship corner of the entire property, was a junk heap of things he no longer wanted but hadn't gotten around to removing. How interesting, I thought: hidden junk in relationships. Using this kind of detective work, see what is revealed about your life through your living space.

Executive Decisions

A very powerful executive asked me to organize his office. A Feng Shui person had visited a few months before. The desk faced the window and a picturesque garden. A mirror had been strategically placed on the desk to let him see who was entering the office. It is preferable to use the Feng Shui cure if the physical problem cannot be remedied. I asked if we might move the desk to the middle of the far-left wall just to see how it looked. We'd position it far enough away from the wall to allow him to sit facing the door. My instincts were right. Now as you entered the room, he was seated at the desk in a position of power. A few days later our paths crossed socially. He told me he couldn't wait to get to work each day. "I feel like I rule the world!"

Feng Shui Cures Revisited

Now that you have a rudimentary understanding of this philosophy and how to apply it, let's look at your exercise sheets once again. On a separate sheet of paper, write down the list of areas to note once again. Beside each one, jot down (if necessary) what you might do to improve the life quality in that area.

- Entrance
- Near-left corner
- Far-left corner
- Left wall connecting the above corners
- Wall straight across from the entrance
- Far-right corner
- Near-right corner
- Right wall connecting the above corners
- The center of the room

Final Note

I hope this taste of Feng Shui makes it a little less foreign and exotic and more understandable and accessible. If these rituals seem strange to you, think how odd the Catholic Mass might look to a visitor from Mars, the dovening of the Jews at the Wailing Wall, or the sight of Muslims on their knees facing Mecca. Every spiritual philosophy has its rituals. Try and embrace the significance of what you are being asked to do rather than getting lost in the newness of the form itself. It is not uncommon for fear to manifest as judgment or anger. Simply note if that has been your response to this information. Remember our goal has been to officially make our homes into sacred spaces. The goal and not the particular modality is of the essence.

正

Zen

CHAPTER 12

Frequently Asked Questions

"Healing is not a destination.
It is a journey.
May this book prove a
worthy companion.
To live life … with dignity,
to celebrate and accept responsibility
for your presence in the world
is all that can be asked of anyone."

—*August Wilson*

Kay Jones was an extraordinary woman, a gifted therapist, and my dear friend. This book is dedicated to her memory as a token of my appreciation for the inestimable contribution she made to my life. For over eight years, I had the good fortune to have a weekly therapy session with Kay. I still share with others many of the wise things she taught me. I thought we would be friends forever. When she and her husband began taking frequent vacations to Montana, I assumed that they would retire there. I was equally sure that time was many years in the future.

Passing the Torch

One day before our session began, Kay told me she had news. She was, in fact, going to retire early. Her house was on the market. She and her family hoped to be in Montana in just a few months. I was stunned. She gently asked me how I felt about this impending change. I thought for only a minute and said without hesitation, "You've shown me how to take care of myself. I'll be okay." And I was. Using the skills she taught me, I arrived at a place in my life where the creation of this book was not only possible, but the next logical step.

There are many things to learn in life. Many teachers have been provided. Through this book, I have become one of yours. You will acquire solid skills within these pages to face all of your organizing challenges. Over time your "organizing muscle" will become strong. You'll be able to tackle a challenge we *haven't* dealt with in this book by modifying a plan of action we *did use* in another area. Remember what Dr. Roberts said? "All knowledge is one."

In the meantime, I've chosen the following topics as being appropriate for our final forum. After you peruse the list, why not take a minute to consider how you'd handle each challenge before you learn what my responses were. The solution will always be some variation on the Eliminate, Categorize, Organize theme. *Those first two tasks are so intertwined, we could flip the first letters and say that mastering this technique makes you the CEO of your life.*

- ♣ Merging households
- ♣ Women's purses
- ♣ The true contents of a briefcase
- ♣ The family car
- ♣ Children who have two home bases
- ♣ Packing a suitcase: personal and business trips

Merging Households: A Case Study

Not long ago I received a call from a former client. Neil lives in the true American West. I had had the good fortune to unpack him in his home several years before. Neil wanted to share some wonderful news. After 40-plus years as a confirmed bachelor, he had found Natalie, the woman of his dreams. Until their marriage, however, they would continue to reside in two different states. Merging the households of two 40-somethings wouldn't be easy under ideal circumstances. They would have duplicates of all the requisite household possessions from toasters to washers and dryers. Now add several hundred miles into the mix. As you can imagine, it was imperative we work as an organized team.

Q: What Are the Most Valuable Considerations in Preparing to Merge Households?

There are two key elements at play when it comes to merging households: careful planning and mutual respect. If one person is moving into the established residence of the other, as was the case here, the person making the move will be under tremendous stress. For example, Natalie was literally dismantling her way of life. She was leaving a home she owned and a city she loved, and she was uprooting two young children. The drama of new schools and new friends was enough to frazzle any parent's peace of mind. Neil's house had to be ready to easily absorb her possessions. On the other hand, the person whose home is doing the absorbing is under another equally powerful kind of stress. Neil would undoubtedly feel displaced with the new arrangement until a period of adjustment has passed. Neil and his fiancée were well-educated professionals who understood these issues. They were unsure how to diffuse the situation and make the transition smoother. I had my work cut out for me.

Q: What Kind of Advance Planning Should I Be Doing?

You don't want to wait until moving day to begin discussing which set of china the new family is going to use. Never make presumptions, by the way, in the area of possessions. You don't want to say, "John, your dishes are so outdated, I just know you'll love using mine," only to discover those outdated dishes are a family heirloom. You can, of course, tell the professional organizer who will try and negotiate on your behalf. "John, I think Becky's dishes work much better in this kitchen than the ones you're using. Could we store yours?" You get the idea.

Each party needs to go through every room in their respective homes and analyze the possessions. I like to think of the new pieces as part of a three-dimensional puzzle. We need to figure out the future of every possession. Keep the lines of communication open, and you'll have less friction.

Here are some of the questions that needed to be answered before my first trip to Neil's house. These pertain to the kitchen and the master suite only. You can alter the questions slightly and apply them to each room of your home.

The Kitchen

❧ How many sets of dishes are in the house to be shared? Will the everyday dishes continue to serve the family? Or would it be more prudent to use the everyday dishes of the incoming party? For example, Neil was using a beautiful set of dishes made of heavy pottery. Natalie has young children. It is easier and safer for young children to use lightweight plastic dinnerware. Neil therefore agreed to pack up his everyday dishes and put them in storage.

If you see some precious items being stored, remember that circumstances change and they may come in handy down the road. You aren't necessarily saying good-bye forever. Here, for example, as the boys matured, heavier dishes would no longer be a problem for them to handle safely, and Neil's dishes could resurface. In addition, Neil and Natalie hope to purchase a weekend home in the mountains one day. Those dishes might come in handy for stocking the weekend kitchen. I'm sure the boys wouldn't mind using paper plates at the mountain retreat.

* Whose dishes will be used for entertaining? We all use the phrase "good china" when referring to the set we use for company. Depending on the storage capacity in the new home, it is likely that only one set will be used and the other packed away. If a couple loves to entertain and a butler's pantry is handy, several sets can be stored comfortably off the dining room. In the spirit of compromise, let me say that even Martha Stewart says she uses mixed patterns on her table.

* The same decisions must be made regarding everyday drinking glasses as well as the glasses (wine, liqueur, and so on) that decorate the table for holidays and other special occasions. Neil had a built-in hutch in the dining room where he stored his extensive collection of glassware. Natalie was bringing her hutch with her, so all of her display items and fancy glassware had an immediate home. In the kitchen, I left half of Neil's everyday glasses for the adults to use and made plastic glasses and paper cups readily available for the children.

* If there is room for a table and chairs, whose will be used? Neil and Natalie had three sets between them. We decided to use hers, store one of his, and donate his second set to charity.

❧ Are there duplicates in prep tools, pots and pans, and cooking machines? Which will be used?

❧ What is the feeling about counter space? Some people cook frequently and want their tools at hand; others want open space in the kitchen. Have you talked about which type you are?

❧ What about the supply of tea towels, aprons, and pot holders?

The Master Suite

❧ Whose towels are going to be used? Merging households is a wonderful opportunity to trash those raggedy towels you have developed a sentimental attachment to or, even better, go out and purchase some new ones to mark the event.

❧ Whose bedding will best suit the décor? These supplies are probably in similar condition as the towels. I say, merge, purge, or splurge.

❧ If you have not weeded through your bathroom paraphernalia yet, now is a wonderful time to do so. Put items in categories and store them in handy containers. Nothing makes one feels less welcome than finding no space for personal items in the bathroom.

❧ Closets are a sticky subject in most merges. Neil has one long closet just outside the master bedroom and another huge closet in the suite itself. I asked him where he thought his intended would be putting her clothing. He thought the hall closet would be perfect. I had his permission to clean it out. I agreed it needed to be reorganized; however, I felt his new wife should have the closet in the bedroom and he should move to the hall. Why?

Because Natalie's children were boys, and, as time passes and they grow to be young men, it would be less embarrassing to catch their stepdad in his underwear than to see their mother in her slip and bra.

Neil agreed in theory, but I knew that emotionally he needed a period of adjustment. For years, he had walked out of the bathroom and gone directly to his closet to get dressed. Now, he would have to make a new groove in the carpet as well as his consciousness. If we made the change now, by the time Natalie arrived two months later, going outside the master suite for his clothes would be second nature.

For the same reason, we moved lots of furniture to storage. Neil would have forgotten what it was like to live with those items by the time Natalie's replacements arrived. Too much change at one time can be cause for friction. We are creatures of habit. You have to be practical when you merge your life with another human being. Love is wonderful, but it isn't enough to handle these fundamental shifts in everyday reality.

Q: Once the Eliminating Has Been Done, What Does One Do with All the Unwanted or Unusable Items?

The possibilities are many. Here are a few suggestions:

- Donate unwanted items to a charity.
- Have a garage sale.
- Give some things to family and friends.
- Rent a storage unit and save some items for future use.
- If your property is big enough, purchase a storage shed.

❧ Store things in the house and, if applicable, rotate the items on a regular basis (here I presume you have storage available in a multicar garage with built-ins or a loft, an attic, or a basement).

The Case of the Empty Boxes

Do you remember the old tags on mattresses? You were warned that it was illegal to remove them. Some consumers would not believe that the warning no longer applied once the mattress was their property. After all, the tag didn't say you could remove it after you made the purchase. It just said it was illegal. Today's consumer may rip off those tags with abandon, but now he's saving the original boxes for all of the electronic equipment he buys. Why? Because he is convinced that the box and packing that arrived with the computer, fax machine, or scanner, is not only perfect, but the only means of transporting this equipment when he moves.

Every home I organize with a sizable investment in equipment has these pesky boxes taking up room somewhere in the house. Nine times out of ten, they are huge and filled with all of the original packing materials. Professional movers can transport your electronic possessions with substitute boxes and adequate padding. If you have purchased a lemon, you'll know within 90 days. Why not compromise and toss the box after the initial three months?

Neil had a two-car garage with a storage loft. It was crammed with empty electronic boxes. Neil would not hear of parting with his original boxes, and we were desperate for space. I suggested we rent a local storage unit so that his wife and stepsons would have room for some of their large-ticket items. Neil compromised: We moved all of the empty boxes to a storage locker and half of the loft was allocated to the new arrivals. When you add up the price of a rental space for a year or two, that's pretty expensive cardboard.

Q: Once the Household Items Have Been Catalogued and Their Ultimate Destinations Decided, What Else Can We Do to Prepare for Move-In Day?

While I had Neil and Natalie examining their possessions from a new perspective, I gave Natalie some additional homework. I asked her to photograph all of the furniture she wanted to bring to the new house and note the dimensions. This way Neil and I would be able to look over her selections and be sure each item fit in its designated spot. Emotions are on the surface the day a moving truck arrives and pours another human being's stuff into an established household. You want to plan ahead and diffuse any possible area of added friction. Here we were eliminating the "why on earth did you think that would fit next to the hutch?" kind of argument.

Compromise Saves the Day

Neil had turned the downstairs den into his office. He is, as you may have gathered, a very serious computer person. As you enter this room, Neil was seated in the middle surrounded by computer monitors, scanners, printers, and the like. I immediately thought of Captain Kirk on the bridge of the *Starship Enterprise*. Natalie had asked Neil to vacate this room. Her valid concern was for her young sons. They had always had a den in which to set up their toys. Natalie felt their bedrooms were for rest and relaxation. If access to the den was denied them, they would be forced to play in their bedrooms or in the very large living room. The latter had always been kept tidy for unexpected company. Before my arrival, Neil had promised he would move his equipment to a smaller room at the end of the hall.

When I saw the room that had been designated as Neil's new home office, my heart sank. I knew immediately this plan was doomed. The room was too small to accommodate all of the computer-related equipment, Neil's multiple file cabinets, and his vast collection of computer programs and games. Captain Kirk would no longer be on the bridge of the *Starship Enterprise;* he'd be toiling in a storage locker. The contents would have to be divided. In addition, there were no phone lines and not enough electrical outlets. Here was an added expense. The room also lacked the same extensive natural light sources of the den.

Remember the "Zen organizing" philosophy? A room should be dedicated to a single purpose. This new arrangement would find Neil forever shuttling between his old den and his new space looking for specific items. I sensed this was fertile breeding ground for resentment. Have you ever heard the phrase "when the honeymoon is over"? When couples are considering major shifts like this one, I ask the person making the change to visualize himself with the new arrangement. How does it feel? Do you think this new arrangement is an improvement? Or do you think you'll be feeling somehow cheated? Let's be realistic; some days we are overworked and tired, and every small inconvenience grates on our nerves. I wanted to de-stress the house, not present the new family with a physical format guaranteed to provoke arguments.

By the way, Neil is rarely playing games on his computer. He directs his business holdings, which are extensive, from his computer. This is a man who needs to have the ideal work area. When we agreed the den would remain his office, Neil compromised elsewhere in the home in favor of the children. His living room would become their after-dinner play area. He was willing to kiss perfect order good-bye in order to keep his office intact. The boys, in turn, promised to pick up if company was expected. Compromise is the soul of a successful multiperson household.

Care of the Silent Ones

If you are merging your life with that of another, I hope you will give great thought and care to helping the silent members of your household make a successful transition. Animals are so often forgotten in all the excitement and hard work at hand. Talk to your vet and to friends with animals who have moved. Gather tips from lots of sources. Here are a few suggestions to give you food for thought. After all, your Fido or Fluffy will have unique needs during this time of transition.

* Tell your pet what is happening and why. Don't just begin dismantling your life. We're all afraid of the unknown, aren't we? Your animal might not understand the exact words you're using, but your tone of voice and demeanor will reassure him or her.

* If they are to live in a new location, be sure you have familiar items to greet them: a favorite toy, their regular food bowls or bed, and so on. This isn't the best time to try a new diet.

* If your animal is to travel without you to the new location, he will be greatly comforted if you can provide an article of clothing with your scent on it.

* A tired dog is less likely to get into trouble. Try not to neglect your regular walks or play time.

* If they are to travel by car, be sure and stop frequently to give your dogs bathroom and exercise breaks. Also, be sure there is adequate room in the vehicle for them.

❧ If your cat is in the car, keep him in his cage. You don't want to take the chance he'll escape. Keep his cage well padded so the floor will be comfortable. Let him have an article of your clothing (I'm thinking old T-shirt here, not Armani jacket!) and a supply of fresh water.

❧ When relocating to a new city, be sure and bring your animal's medical history for your new vet.

❧ Don't forget to legally resister your pet with the local authorities.

❧ Neil and Natalie both had dogs. They were sure to introduce their pets months before they got married. Some animals are extremely territorial and you want to integrate new housemates gradually and respectfully.

❧ Finally, consider a few drops of the Bach Flower Remedy called Rescue Remedy (available at your local health food store) in your pet's water. Start about two weeks before the commotion begins and continue until a few weeks after the new routine has been established. In a really tough transition, you can put the drops directly under the animal's tongue.

A Woman's Purse

I discovered recently that some men find an organized purse to be sexy. Ladies, I share this with you as an added incentive to toss half that stuff you're carrying. I used to haul an enormous purse around with me wherever I went. As women, we derive a sense of security knowing we have every single item with us that could possibly be needed in this lifetime. Right about now, somewhere a woman is saying, "Just the other day someone needed a Phillips-head screwdriver and I just happened to have one. If I cleaned out my purse, I wouldn't have been able to save the day." It's true. You have a choice: Save the day or save your body. Let me explain.

One day, my chiropractor looked at my purse and strolled over to it. Arnold Schwarzenegger could have used my bag to build his biceps. My doctor picked up my purse, grimaced, and then turned to me and said, "You need to take this weight off your neck." It took me a few weeks to get with the program and wean myself off the Big Bag syndrome. I'm here to tell you that good things come in small packages.

Q: What Does a Woman Absolutely Need to Carry?

- Lipstick, a compact, a nail file, two Band-Aids, some tissues
- A comb or a small brush
- House keys
- Photo ID
- Next of kin card
- Pertinent medical info, if needed (in the case of a diabetic or someone with drug allergies, for example)
- One major credit card
- Checkbook and pen
- A small change purse for coins and some cash
- A small notepad for miscellaneous note taking

What a Woman Also Needs If She Owns a Car

- Car keys
- Driver's license (in many states this will have a photo)
- A gas card

Some Additional Items Some Women May Find Indispensable

- ❧ A beeper
- ❧ A cellular phone

I wear a beeper and use it in place of a watch. My beeper has eliminated the perpetual suntan line I had on my wrist. I have a cell phone, but leave it in my car for emergencies only. If I lived in a large city, I'd probably want to tuck a phone into my purse. Try to purchase the smallest, lightest phone available. One of my clients has a phone the size of a pack of cigarettes.

Ye Olde Canvas Bag

From time to time, a woman will have additional items she needs to take with her. These can go into one of those canvas bags we all seem to collect. Today, for example, I'll take a break from writing and drive to Chinatown to stock up on herbs. I toss my empty bottles into my canvas bag and bring home the refills. Pare your tote bag collection down to a favorite and a spare.

Q: What Key Elements Keep a Purse Organized?

The secret to keeping your purse organized is two-fold. First you should purchase a bag that has compartments. For example, I don't carry a makeup case, but I do keep my compact and lipstick isolated from my checkbook. This saves time when I need to retrieve an item quickly. I don't like a huge wallet that isolates every valuable you are carrying into one tidy bundle a thief can grab. I keep enough cash for the day in a small zippered compartment in my purse with my ID. If I think I may need additional funds, it will be stored elsewhere in my bag or on my person.

The second element that will keep your purse tidy is cleaning it out *every* day. Pull out all those slips of papers with notes and phone numbers on them. Either transfer the information where you'll need to find it in the future (computer, address book, calendar, and so on) or file it in your To Do folder. Be sure and file your receipts as well.

Find a home for all the extraneous items that floated into your purse today. Your child's half-eaten candy bar can go in the trash, that perfume sample they handed you as you exited the store can be tossed or taken to the bathroom, and so on.

The Briefcase

I have observed three types of briefcase users:

- Our first type is the person who actually uses the briefcase to transport work either to and from the office or on business trips.

- Our second type has no idea what a briefcase is for, so you usually find miscellaneous items like candy bars, newspapers, and crossword puzzles inside.

- Our last intrepid businessperson overloads his briefcase, transporting every imaginable document everywhere he goes "just in case" it's ever needed. His back is breaking, his shoulders and neck are in spasm, and he's chronically exhausted. He is also, in his mind, prepared. A good scout traveling down the wrong road.

Q: Okay, I Give Up. What Should I Be Putting in My Briefcase?

Let's start with a blank slate. Empty everything from your briefcase. Let's look at the briefcase itself. Does it please you?

Do you like the color? Did you treat yourself to something especially beautiful? Nonverbal communication extends to our possessions as much as it is reflected in what we wear. Carry a briefcase that not only pleases you, but one that speaks volumes about you the minute you make an appearance.

Now, let's follow our time-honored three-step formula. *Eliminate* everything you really don't need. Put the business papers you do need to save in *categories* as you work the elimination process. Now, we're ready to *Zen organize* your briefcase. Ask yourself the following questions to help move things along:

- Do any of the papers I have decided to save actually belong in files I now keep in my home or office? File them appropriately.

- Are some of the papers related to projects I no longer work on in multiple locations? File these papers in the one location where you will need them. Contractors, for example, may carry papers to and from locations until the project is completed.

- There are wonderful electronic aids that are compatible with one's computer. You can have access to all your stored information in the palm of your hand.

- You can carry multiple documents on disk. One of my clients has a fabulous toy, a portable printer the size of a carton of cigarettes.

- Once you are online, you can have documents e-mailed to you wherever you are in the world.

These suggestions all work in concert with the information presented in Chapter 3, "The Work Space."

The Family Car

Q: What Do I Absolutely Need in the Trunk of My Car?

- A tool kit (car jack and so on).
- A spare tire.
- Flares.
- Motor oil.
- Earthquake kit (if applicable).
- Emergency food and water (one bottle for human consumption and one in case your car gets thirsty!).
- Extra pair of walking shoes.
- A warm sweater or jacket.
- One umbrella.
- If you have a dog, you'll want to carry an extra bowl and some emergency cans of food.

The businessperson may also want to carry …

- A portable file case to have paper supplies at hand. This is especially true in professions where one has forms to fill out, such as in the insurance or real estate fields.
- Another small container can house everyday office supplies that might come in handy when processing forms, such as a stapler and refills, paper clips, tape, a few extra pencils and pens, and so on.

Every person must tailor the list to suit his or her individual needs and personality. For example, when my parents retired to the country, they never drove more than a few miles from home and they never set out in inclement weather. A stash of food and water would have been taking up space. As a resident of Los Angeles, I drive many miles every day to see clients. If the traffic on the freeway becomes jammed, my arrival home will be delayed. I always carry a health food bar or a piece of fruit so that I can keep my blood sugar elevated. I also have a case of water in my trunk. Living in California, this is an integral part of my earthquake safety. If you live in an area that is prone to natural disasters like earthquakes, consider having survival provisions in your vehicle.

Q: What About the Glove Compartment?

Here I would carry the essentials:

- Legal papers pertaining to the car
- Maps
- Instructions for handling an accident

Q: What About a Child's Needs in the Car?

The number of diversions for a child should be in direct proportion to the length of time you predict the trip will take. There are storage containers with compartments that hook on to the backs of the front seats. You can stash books, soft toys, and other diversions here. A young child may be comforted by his or her favorite stuffed animal; an older child can become absorbed by a Game Boy.

Q: How Does One Manage the Physical Needs of Children of Divorce?

There are two key considerations:

- The physical needs of the child in both locations
- Good communication between the parents

Q: How Do We Assess the Physical Needs of the Child?

The following points can head you in the right direction.

- A child needs an adequate number of toys in the home he most frequently visits. It needn't be as extensive as the one he has at his home base. Each location can be made special by the unique play items available.

- If school nights are divided between both parents, provisions should be made for school supplies and teaching aids.

- Most children pack a small suitcase for the visit. It's nice to have extra sets of the basics: underwear, PJs, T-shirts, socks, sweats, and exercise shoes. It's nice, too, to have an extra dress outfit for spur-of-the-moment invitations. I know a devoted father who wanted to take his children to church one Sunday, but their dress clothes were all at his ex-wife's. A little planning would have enabled them to worship together.

If there is good communication between the parents about the items present in each home and the ever-changing needs of the child, things should not only run smoothly, but money can be saved.

Packing a Suitcase: The Basics

Q: What's the Best Suitcase to Travel With?

Without picking a particular brand name, I'd have to say that unless you have a very active social life at your destination, one small suitcase with wheels that will fit in the overhead bin on a plane is adequate for most travel. I once traveled for 10 weeks with such a bag. It was summer and I became quite adept at hand-washing those no-wrinkle rayon frocks I tucked everywhere. The key elements here are the wheels and the fact that you can bypass checking your luggage.

Q: How Do I Decide What Clothes I'll Need?

I am a visual person, so sometimes I create a document like the one that follows to help me get control over a situation. Other times, I find I can do the planning in my head. What's the difference? If you invite me to spend the weekend with you, I will probably not need to write things down as I have spent a lifetime traveling to friends' homes for the weekend. On the other hand, if you ask me to be one the speakers at a conference in London in January, I'll want to chart everything because there is a dual purpose to the trip and a change of climate. Please don't feel restricted by the following exercise. It is meant to be a tool if you need help. Grab some paper and a pencil, and follow these steps:

1. On the top half of the paper, write out the days of the week you'll be traveling. You'll want to do this in calendar style the way we worked on our schedules in Chapter 3.

2. Write in the name of the city, where you'll be staying (a hotel or with family or friends), and the main activities of the day (sightseeing, state dinner at the White House, or picnic with the folks). Leave room for more information.

3. Now, on the lower half of the paper, write out a list of every single garment you would like to take with you.

Be sure to include outfits for travel days. Airlines recommend pants for ladies and flats in the event you might have to go down an emergency slide.

4. Let's return to the top of the page. Start with the one outfit you won't leave home without. Put it on the calendar on a day you know it will be perfect. Now, before you add a second outfit, ask yourself who is going to see you the first day you wear your treasured clothes? Will they see you again? (Your mother doesn't count, and neither do hotel employees or cab drivers.) Let's see what other days we could wear this outfit. Write this outfit in again on another day or two.

5. Continue writing in outfits on the calendar. Be sure to mark them off in the following section.

6. Now that you have a few days filled in, remember your travel clothes. Slacks and a top or sweater (depending on the season) can be worn in the city you're traveling to as an outfit. You can increase the value by taking a few extra tops. Let's say you're wearing a pair of slacks and a top. Take another top suitable for those slacks. And take a skirt that can be worn with both tops. Voilà! You now have at least four outfits! If your original outfit is a skirt and blouse, break the outfit and mix 'n' match it as well.

7. Take no more than three pairs of shoes: the ones you're wearing to travel, another suitable for all outfits and walking if necessary, and a third pair if a dressy occasion is on the agenda.

Take a look at an example of a "packing calendar."

Trip to Memphis in August

	Wednesday	Thursday	Friday	Saturday
	Fly to Memphis	Day: Meeting/ client	Day: Sight- seeing	Fly home
Stay with friends	Eve.: Dinner/ theater	Eve.: Dinner/ friends	Eve.: Dinner/ friends	
	Outfit #1	Outfit #2— Day	Outfit #1— Day	Outfit #1
	Sweatshirt Jeans Walking shoes	Blue pantsuit White blouse Blue shoes	Red sweater Jeans Walking shoes	Sweatshirt Jeans Walking shoes
		Outfit #3— Eve.	Outfit #2— Eve.	
		Black dress Black high- heeled shoes	Blue pantsuit Light-blue blouse Blue shoes	

For all days: Raincoat with zip-out lining

Clothes I'd like to take:

White blouse	Jeans	Black dress
Light-blue blouse	~~Black pants~~	~~Flower print dress~~
Red sweater	Blue pantsuit	
~~Yellow sweater set~~	~~Shorts~~	Black high-heeled shoes
		~~Boots~~
		Walking shoes

The Story of the Frequent Flyer

Samantha is one of those business people who is on the go all the time. Sam called me a few months after I organized her master bedroom closet. She wondered if I could help her select her wardrobe for an upcoming trip. Let's take a look at the chart we designed for this trip. It will help you create one for your travels. Sam, by the way, can now plan for these trips in her head. She told me that using a written chart for about six months gave her the courage to take less when she traveled.

Samantha's trip was a combination of business and pleasure over a long weekend in New York City. She was traveling in late October, a time when you begin to feel a chill in the air on the East Coast. We'd have to get her winter clothes out of their Los Angeles hiding places to accommodate her journey's needs. I questioned Sam about her trip. What was the purpose? Who would she see? Was she traveling alone? Would she see the same business colleagues at several functions? Here is what I discovered:

- Sam was to leave on Thursday night on the red-eye. She would return on Sunday around 6 P.M. from JFK to LAX. Her husband was staying home and she would be traveling alone.

- The business highlight was a dinner at a large hotel in midtown Manhattan on Saturday night. Although not a formal affair, she would need to dress up a bit. This was a function for several hundred people to honor the top executive at one of the firms that Sam did business with on a regular basis.

- On Friday and Sunday (until her departure), she was free to meet with friends and planned to go to the Metropolitan Museum, take in a Broadway show, and eat out at least once at a good restaurant.

I asked Sam to lay out on her bed every outfit she planned to take. This is the physical equivalent of making that wish list I suggested. When I looked at the sea of clothes Sam wanted to take, I questioned her about each item. Here is what I knew based on her itinerary:

- 🏵 Traveling on the red-eye required loose, extremely comfortable clothes. If the flight was not full, she might score several seats together. I like to lift up the arm rests and sleep as we cross the country.

- 🏵 The clothes Sam wore to the Saturday night dinner would serve her well at the theatre on Friday night. She was meeting friends who were not involved in her business life. The outfit would, therefore, be new to both groups of people.

- 🏵 The same outfit she would wear to go to the museum would be fine for Sunday brunch or sightseeing.

Here's what our chart looked like:

Trip to New York

Thursday	Friday	Saturday	Sunday
Fly to NYC	Day: Met. museum	Day: Sightseeing	Day: Shopping
Check in hotel	Eve.: Dinner/ theater	Eve.: Formal dinner	Fly home
Outfit #1	Outfit #2—Day	Outfit #2—Day	Outfit #1
Sweatshirt	Light wool pantsuit	Light wool pantsuit	Wool pantsuit
Jeans	White blouse	Blue blouse	White blouse
Walking shoes	Casual shoes	Casual shoes	Casual shoes

Thursday	Friday	Saturday	Sunday
	Outfit #3—Eve.	Outfit #2—Eve.	Outfit #1
	Black dress	Black dress	Afternoon
	Black high-heeled shoes	Black high-heeled shoes	Sweatshirt
			Jeans
			Walking shoes

For all days, she needed a raincoat with zip-out lining, an evening purse, and a woolen shawl.

Q: What About Toiletries? They Seem to Take Up So Much Room!

Make a list of every cosmetic, shampoo and conditioner, and skin-care product you need or use on a daily basis. Most manufacturers sell scaled-down versions of their products for travel. Alternatively, you can go to your local drugstore and purchase travel bottles. Put the needed products in these containers and label them using the label machine you purchased for your office. Purchase a hanging toiletries bag at the store while you're there. If counter space is at a premium at your destination, you can maneuver easily.

You might be interested to know that our friend Sam made a list of her travel toiletries and I had the sheet laminated. She keeps it in her suitcase and uses it as a checklist before she leaves home. Sam finds it comes in handy on trips that involve multiple stops. Gathering together all of your possessions is a no-brainer when all you have to do is check them against a list.

I have long observed the clever time-saver a man's shaving kit represents. Every man I know who travels keeps a kit in his suitcase with spare supplies. I suggest you do the same if you are a woman who travels. Keep a travel bag packed at all times with your cosmetic needs ready to go.

Q: Are There Any Other Products I Should Invest in for Travel Purposes?

There are wonderful items out there and you really should investigate and match up what is available with your personal needs. Here are a few I personally enjoy:

- A blow-up pillow for my neck to make long flights more comfortable. Airline pillows are notorious for being unsanitary. Another choice is to have your own small pillowcase for the airline pillow provided.

- Small, lightweight, powerful hair dryers are on the marketplace. If you're traveling with someone, only one of you needs to bring the hair dryer.

- A small steam iron will take wrinkles out of clothes at your destination.

- I always have a small travel alarm with me. I don't want to depend on the hotel operator, and friends usually have complicated bedside clocks.

- A small mending kit is helpful.

- If you're doing a lot of sightseeing, bring a folded bag with you. You can fill this with your purchases and carry it on the plane to be stored under the seat in front. Anything too big for this bag should be shipped home.

- Don't forget your prescription medications and carry an extra pair of contacts or eyeglasses.

Q: How Do I Assemble Everything?

Place everything in categories: clothes in one area, "stuff" in another, and toiletries in a third. It's easiest to work on your bed.

- Place your "stuff" on the bottom, remembering that when you pick up the suitcase, everything falls toward the bottom. Better to have the steam iron and the hair dryer go flying than your cashmere sweater. Place the hanging bag with your toiletries here as well. Don't want to buy one? Use large plastic resealable bags from your kitchen. Keep things in categories: nighttime products, makeup, hair care, and so on.

- Now on this foundation, place your folded clothes. Some of these rolling bags come with a shelf you can place the clothes on. You can use a piece of sturdy cardboard if your suitcase didn't come with one.

- In the outside pockets, place the items you need to grab on the plane: the pillow, a small travel umbrella, and so on.

- I like to keep my tickets, money, and all other necessary valuables on my person or in my purse.

Q: Any Final Words of Wisdom?

- Be sure that everything you're taking is an old friend. By that I mean, don't fly to Europe and discover at Heathrow that your shoes don't fit after 10 minutes of walking or your slacks leave no room for expansion after a big meal.

- As for toiletries, tuck in some toilet paper and soap if you're going abroad. You can purchase just about anything you'll need anywhere in the world. I remember one day I was nervous about a business trip I was about to take. My assistant was taking me to LAX. I told her I needed to stop at the corner store to pick up some breath mints. She looked at me like I was insane and said sweetly, "Regina, I just bet they sell breath mints in New York City."

❧ Remember to secure your home environment. Be sure to have a neighbor pick up your newspaper, have the lights on timers, and be sure the alarm is set.

❧ Leaving someone with your children or pets? Why not make a laminated sheet explaining how you want everyone to be taken care of. With each trip you will only have to plug in the details of your itinerary. Be sure and leave your contact numbers while traveling as well as those of helpful contacts at home.

Business Travel

Q: Your Notes on Packing Were Helpful, But What About the Business Traveler? We're Going to Have to Carry More Items. How Do We Keep Control over Everything?

Your basic needs will be the same no matter what the destination or purpose for the trip. However, the business traveler is going to have one or two formal outfits. The best solution is taking along one additional bag, specifically a hanging bag. These bags usually have outside pockets that can easily accommodate the added accoutrements (formal shoes and so on) necessitated by the business wardrobe items you'll be wearing.

The Other Side of the Coin

Questions are an interesting phenomenon. When I give my students a specific assignment, they inevitably ask questions that pertain to carrying out the exercise. If I allow hands to go up during the lecture, the forward motion of the class frequently comes to a screeching halt. The vast majority of questions are not about clarification. Questions often reveal deep-seated fears. The questioner unconsciously wants to derail the proceedings. I want to point this out to you because some of you have purchased this book as a way of getting out of becoming organized. "Look," you shout at your spouse, roommate, parent, or dog, "this author thinks *I* have the time to do this! Is she crazy? I bought the book and it doesn't work. I just can't be organized." There are several variations on this theme, but you get the idea. If you recognize yourself here, try and face the fears behind this type of negative patter. *You have the power not only to change, but to decide when it happens.* Being organized does not guarantee the best job or the most envied spouse, nor will it whiten your teeth. It simply guarantees that your life can be lived more easily and joyously. If you didn't want that ease and joy in your life, you wouldn't be reading this book.

Final Note

I know that *The Zen of Organizing* will give you the information you need to start your organizing adventure. Every time a negative thought enters your mind about your ability to succeed, picture me standing next to you saying, "Nonsense! Of course, you can do this!" I am your personal cheerleader (albeit not in a short skirt, go-go boots, or midriff top). If it still seems impossible, go back to the beginning of this book and start with the basic steps. If you have to do that 1,000 times, it doesn't matter. Showing up to make the attempt is a triumph all by itself.

All professional organizers are teaching the same material. Each of us simply has a different approach. You may be deeply impacted by something I say and not understand the exact same piece of information when it is expressed by another professional organizer. I hope you will proceed with patience, love, and respect for yourself as well as for the work at hand. We are here to learn. Every challenge that is met is replaced by a new challenge for us to face. It is the nature of life on this planet. It happens that an organized life will help you better face every challenge heading in your direction. If I could personally inscribe your copy of *The Zen of Organizing*, here is what I would write:

> *"Healing is not a destination.*
> *It is a journey.*
> *May this book prove a*
> *worthy companion."*

*"Go in peace.
The mission you are on
is under the eye of the Lord."*

—Judges 18:6

Index

A

action files, 48
ADD (Attention Deficit Disorder), as hindrance to organization, 154
advance planning
  merging households, 204
  moving, 175-177
album storage, organizing common rooms, 118
alphabetizing music selections, 117
animals/pets, merging households, 211-212
archival files, 51
Attention Deficit Disorder. *See* ADD

B

baby clothes, parting with, 73
baby rooms, creative solutions for, 141-142
bagua, Feng Shui, 188-191
bathroom organization, 81
  checklist, 90-91
  clearing the way, 84
  creating a retreat, 82-83
  drawer liners, 85
  shelf creators, 86-88
  small spaces, 92
  storing of items, 88-93
  under the sink, 85-86
  zip-lock bags, 88
bedroom organization, merging households, 206-207
Black Hat Sect, Feng Shui, 187
book storage, organizing common rooms, 120-123
box bottom hanging files, 43-44
"brain dance," 4

briefcase organization, contents, 215-216
burning incense, creating sacred space, 186
burning sage sticks, creating sacred space, 186
business travel, 228

C

cabinets. *See* cupboards
can dispensers, kitchen organization, 105
car organization
  children's needs, 218-219
  glove compartment, 218
  trunk, 217-218
cassette storage, 119-120
catalogues, organizing common rooms, 130
categories
  files, 47
    action files, 48
    recipes, 49-50
    travel articles, 49
  food, kitchen organization, 102-103
    can dispensers, 105
    glass containers, 105
    labeled shelves, 103
    shelf baskets, 104
    shelf creators, 103
    shelf dividers, 103
    zip-lock bags, 105
  moving, 177
  music selections, 118-119
CD storage, 119-120
change (reality of), 166
chi (Chinese word for "energy"), 186-188

children's rooms (organization), 137
　baby and toddler tips, 141-142
　childhood memorabilia, 145
　creative solutions for furniture,
　　140-141
　nurturing children through the envi-
　　ronment, 137-140
　teenage rooms, 144
　young child's room, 142-144
Chinese techniques, Feng Shui, 186-187
　bagua, 188-191
　Black Hat Sect, 187
　compass school, 187
　cures, 191-198
　exercise, 195-196
　revelations about your life through liv-
　　ing space, 197
chronic fatigue syndrome, as hindrance to
　organization, 155
closet organization, 69
　checklist, 74-75
　clothing of the deceased, 77-78
　design, 75-77
　fake prosperity, 74
　hall closets, 131
　life stories, 70-72
　parting with baby clothes, 73
　purging, 73
　size wars, 73
clothing of the deceased, 77-78
collectibles, adding personal touch to
　common rooms, 132
color
　adding personal touch to common
　　rooms, 133
　coding files, 45, 47
command stations, kitchen organization,
　99
　division by task, 100-101
common rooms, 115
　hall closets, 131
　house rules for pets, 134
　living rooms
　　books, 120-123
　　creativity, 128
　　magazines and catalogues, 130
　　memorabilia, 128-130
　　music, 117-120
　　photo albums, 124-128
　　videos, 123-124
　　what your living room says about you,
　　　116-117
　office space, 115

personal touches, 131
　collectibles, 132
　color, 133
　fragrance, 133
　lighting, 133
　pictures, 132
　plants, 133
communication, dealing with instant,
　63-64
compass school, Feng Shui, 187
compromise, merging households, 209,
　211
concept of energy, Feng Shui, 186-187
　bagua, 188-191
　Black Hat Sect, 187
　compass school, 187
　cures, 191-198
　exercise, 195-196
　revelations about your life through liv-
　　ing space, 197
cookbooks, storage of, 110
counter space, kitchen organization,
　107-108
creative visualization, 9
cupboards, 97-99
cures, Feng Shui, 191-198

D

deceased, clothing of, 77-78
decorations, seasonal, 111
delegating tasks, 30-31
depression, as hindrance to organization,
　156-157
　antidotes for, 157-158
design, closets, 75-77
designating a purpose for the home office,
　58
displaying
　dishes, kitchen organization, 110-111
　glasses, kitchen organization, 111
dot technique, moving, 179-180
drawers
　junk drawer, kitchen organization, 106
　liners, 85
　"macho" drawer, kitchen organization,
　　105
　miscellaneous drawers, kitchen organi-
　　zation, 106

E

eliminating (first step to organization), 10
emotional ties to chaos, 149-155
  ADD, 154
  chronic fatigue syndrome, 155
  depression, 156-157
    antidotes for, 157-158
    fear, 158
  success and failure, 158-161
    open-door policy, 159-160
  ending the cycle, 152-153
  peri-menopause, 154-155
  substance abuse, 153
empty boxes, merging households,
  208-209
energy, Feng Shui, 186-187
  bagua, 188-191
  Black Hat Sect, 187
  compass school, 187
  cures, 191-198
  exercise, 195-196
  revelations about your life through liv-
    ing space, 197
environment maintenance, 168-169
Epstein-Barr virus. *See* chronic fatigue
  syndrome
exercise, Feng Shui, 195-196

F

fear, as hindrance to organization, 158
  success and failure, 158-161
Feng Shui (ancient art of placement), 187
  creating sacred space, 186-187
    bagua, 188-191
    Black Hat Sect, 187
    compass school, 187
    cures, 191-198
    exercise, 195-196
    *revelations about your life through liv-
      ing space, 197*
files, 42
  archival files, 51
  categories, 47
    action files, 48
    recipes, 49-50
    travel articles, 49
  color-coding, 45-47
  hanging files
    box bottom, 43-44
    tabs, 45
  improving existing files, 51-52

one piece of paper at a time, 47
  placement of the filing cabinet, 53
  purging files, 52
  related files, 43
  setting up new files, 50-51
finding movers, 174-175
food storage, kitchen organization, 102
  can dispensers, 105
  categories of food, 102-103
  glass containers, 105
  labeled shelves, 103
  shelf baskets, 104
  shelf creators, 103
  shelf dividers, 103
  zip-lock bags, 105
fountains, Feng Shui, 190
fragrance, adding personal touch to common rooms, 133
frequent flyers, suitcase organization,
  223-225
frequently asked questions, 201
  briefcases, contents of, 215-216
  business travel, 228
  family car
    children's needs, 218-219
    glove compartment, 218
    trunk, 217-218
  merging households, 203
    advanced planning, 204
    animals/pets, 211-212
    compromise, 209-211
    empty boxes, 208-209
    kitchen, 204-206
    master suite, 206-207
    move-in day, 209
    unwanted items, 207-208
  suitcases
    assembliing everything, 227
    choosing a suitcase, 219
    *deciding what clothes are necessary,
      220-221*
    frequent flyers, 223-225
    "packing calendar," 222
    toiletries, 225-226
    travel products, 226
  woman's purse, 212
    compartmentalized bags, 214-215
    necessities, 213-214
furniture
  children's rooms, 140-141
  home office setup, 54-55

G

glass containers, kitchen organization, 105
glasses, displaying, kitchen organization, 111
glove compartment organization, 218
goals, 8-9
  exercise, 22-25
  matching with schedules, 26
  caring for physical self, 26-28
  delegating, 30-31
  hiring help, 31-32
  overbooking, 28-30

H

hall closet organization, 131
hanging files
  box bottom, 43-44
  tabs, 45
hiring help, 31-32
holiday gift planning, 34-35
holiday party planning, 36-37
home office, 57
  dealing with instant communication, 63-64
  designating a purpose, 58
  furniture setup, 54-55
  improving working conditions, 58-60
  in-and-out boxes, 60-61
  size considerations, 61
  marriage to physical drama of chaotic work life, 65-66
  paying bills, 62-63
  resistance to change, 66-67

I–J

imagination, exercising yours, 10
in-and-out boxes, 60-61
  size considerations, 61
instant communication, 63-64

junior crates, 85
junk drawer, kitchen organization, 106

K

kitchen organization, 98
  command stations, 99
  division by task, 100-101
  counter space, 107-108

creating atmosphere
  lighting, 110
  plants, 109
cupboards, 97-99
displaying dishes, 110-111
displaying glasses, 111
food storage, 102
  can dispensers, 105
  categories of food, 102-103
  glass containers, 105
  labeled shelves, 103
  shelf baskets, 104
  shelf creators, 103
  shelf dividers, 103
  zip-lock bags, 105
junk drawer, 106
"macho" drawer, 105
merging households, 204-206
miscellaneous drawers, 106
one-step stools, 102
refrigerator top, 110
seasonal decorations, 111
spices, storage ideas, 107-108
under the sink, 108-109
wine storage, 110

L

labeled shelves, kitchen organization, 103
life pie chart (exercise), 19-22
lighting
  adding personal touch to common rooms, 133
  creating atmosphere in kitchens, 110
liners, drawer, 85
living rooms
  book storage, 120-123
  creativity, 128
  magazines and catalogues, 130
  memorabilia, 128-130
  organizing music, 117
    album storage, 118
    alphabetizing, 117
    containers for CDs, cassettes, and VHS tapes, 119-120
    division by categories, 118-119
    master computer lists, 117
  photo albums, 124-128
  video storage, 123-124
  what your living room says about you, 116-117

M

"macho" drawer, kitchen organization, 105
magazines, organizing common rooms, 130
magic formula for success, 10
  categorize, 11
  eliminate, 10
  organize, 11
maintenance, 166-173
  creating a habit, 169-170
  environment, 168-169
managing time, 15
  dealing with frantic activity, 32
  goals and wishes exercise, 22-25
  holiday gift planning, 34-35
  holiday party planning, 36-37
  life pie chart, 19, 22
  matching goals with schedules, 26
    caring for physical self, 26-28
    delegating, 30-31
    hiring help, 31-32
    overbooking, 28, 30
  reasons to get organized exercise, 16-19
  wish lists, 32
master computer lists, music selections, 117
memorabilia
  childhood, 145
  organizing common rooms, 128-130
merging households, frequently asked questions, 203
  advanced planning, 204
  animals/pets, 211-212
  compromise, 209, 211
  empty boxes, 208-209
  kitchen, 204-206
  master suite, 206-207
  move-in day, 209
  unwanted items, 207-208
miscellaneous drawers, kitchen organization, 106
moving
  move-in day, merging households, 209
  preparation, 173
    advance planning, 175-177
    categorizing items, 177
    dot technique, 179-180
    eliminating what you do not need, 177
    finding movers, 174-175
    new location preparations, 180-181
    organizing the move, 177-179
music organization, 117
  album storage, 118
  alphabetizing, 117
  containers for CDs, cassettes, and VHS tapes, 119-120
  division by categories, 118-119
  master computer lists, 117

N–O

nurturing children through the environment, 137-140

office space, 115
one-step stools, kitchen organization, 102
open-door policy, 159-160
overbooking schedules, 28-30

P

"packing calendar," suitcase organization, 222
pantry, kitchen organization, 102
  can dispensers, 105
  categories of food, 102-103
  glass containers, 105
  labeled shelves, 103
  shelf baskets, 104
  shelf creators, 103
  shelf dividers, 103
  zip-lock bags, 105
paying bills, 62-63
peri-menopause, as hindrance to organization, 154-155
personal touches, 131
  collectibles, 132
  color, 133
  fragrance, 133
  lighting, 133
  pictures, 132
  plants, 133
pets, house rules, 134
photo albums, organizing common rooms, 124-128
physical ties to chaos, 149-155
  ADD, 154
  chronic fatigue syndrome, 155
  depression, 156-157
    antidotes for, 157-158
    fear, 158
  success and failure, 158-161
    open-door policy, 159-160
  ending the cycle, 152-153
  peri-menopause, 154-155
  substance abuse, 153
pictures, adding personal touch to common rooms, 132
placement of the filing cabinet, 53

plants
  adding personal touch to common
    rooms, 133
  creating atmosphere in kitchens, 109
  Feng Shui, 191
preparations for moving, 173
  advance planning, 175-177
  categorizing items, 177
  dot technique, 179-180
  eliminating what you do not need, 177
  finding movers, 174-175
  new location preparations, 180-181
  organizing the move, 177-179
prosperity corner (Feng Shui), 189
purging
  closets, 73
  files, 52
purse organization, 212
  compartmentalized bags, 214-215
  necessities, 213-214

Q

questions (frequently asked questions),
  201
  briefcases, contents, 215-216
  business travel, 228
  family car
    children's needs, 218-219
    glove compartment, 218
    trunk, 217-218
  merging households, 203
    advanced planning, 204
    animals/pets, 211-212
    compromise, 209-211
    empty boxes, 208-209
    kitchen, 204-206
    master suite, 206-207
    move-in day, 209
    unwanted items, 207-208
  suitcases
    assembling everything, 227
    choosing a suitcase, 219
    deciding what clothes are necessary,
      220-221
    frequent flyers, 223-225
    "packing calendar," 222
    toiletries, 225-226
    travel products, 226
  woman's purse, 212
    compartmentalized bags, 214-215
    necessities, 213-214

R

reasons to get organized (exercise), 16-19
refrigerator top, kitchen organization, 110
related files, 43
revelations about your life through living
  space, Feng Shui, 197

S

sacred space, creating, 185-186
scheduling, 26
  caring for physical self first, 26-28
  delegating, 30-31
  hiring help, 31-32
  overbooking, 28-30
seasonal decorations, kitchen organization, 111
setting up new files, 50-51
shelf baskets, kitchen organization, 104
shelf creators
  bathroom organization, 86-88
  kitchen organization, 103
shelf dividers, kitchen organization, 103
sink (under the sink solutions), 85-86
small spaces, bathroom organization, 92
spices, kitchen organization, storage ideas,
  107-108
steps to organization, 10
  categorize, 11
  eliminate, 10
  organize, 11
storage
  albums, organizing common rooms,
    118
  bathroom organization, 88-93
  CDs, cassettes, and VHS tapes, 119-120
  cookbooks, 110
  food, 102
    can dispensers, 105
    categories of food, 102-103
    glass containers, 105
    labeled shelves, 103
    shelf baskets, 104
    shelf creators, 103
    shelf dividers, 103
    zip-lock bags, 105
  memorabilia, 128-130
  spices, kitchen organization, 107-108
  wine, kitchen organization, 110
substance abuse, as hindrance to organization, 153

successful magic formula, 10
 categorize, 11
 eliminate, 10
 organize, 11
suitcase organization
 assembliing everything, 227
 choosing a suitcase, 219
 deciding what clothes are necessary, 220-221
 frequent flyers, 223-225
 "packing calendar," 222
 toiletries, 225-226
 travel products, 226

T

tabs (hanging files), 45
teenager's rooms, creative solutions, 144
time management, 15
 dealing with frantic activity, 32
 goals and wishes exercise, 22-25
 holiday gift planning, 34-35
 holiday party planning, 36-37
 life pie chart, 19-22
 matching goals with schedules, 26
  caring for physical self, 26-28
  delegating, 30-31
  hiring help, 31-32
  overbooking, 28-30
 reasons to get organized (exercise), 16-19
 wish lists, 32
toddler rooms, creative solutions, 141-142
toiletries, suitcase organization, 225-226
travel products, suitcase organization, 226
trunk organization, 217-218

U

under the sink solutions, 85-86, 108-109
unwanted items, merging households, 207-208
use of time, 15
 dealing with frantic activity, 32
 goals and wishes exercise, 22-25
 holiday gift planning, 34-35
 holiday party planning, 36-37
 life pie chart, 19-22
 matching goals with schedules, 26
  caring for physical self, 26-28
  delegating, 30-31
  hiring help, 31-32
  overbooking, 28-30
 reasons to get organized exercise, 16-19
 wish lists, 32

V–W

VHS tapes storage, 119-120
video storage, organizing common rooms, 123-124

wine storage, kitchen organization, 110
woman's purse, 212
 compartmentalized bags, 214-215
 necessities, 213-214
work space, 40-42
 basic furniture setup for home office, 54-55
 computers, 55-56
 files, 42
  archival, 51
  categories, 47-50
  color-coding, 45-47
  hanging, 43-44
  improving existing, 51-52
  one piece of paper at a time, 47
  placement of the filing cabinet, 53
  purging, 52
  related, 43
  setting up new, 50-51
  tabs, 45
 home office arrangement, 57
  dealing with instant communication, 63-64
  designating a purpose, 58
  improving working conditions, 58-60
  in-and-out boxes, 60-61
  marriage to physical drama of chaotic work life, 65-66
  paying bills, 62-63
  resistance to change, 66-67

X–Y–Z

young children's rooms, creative solutions, 142-144

zip-lock bags
 bathroom organization, 88
 kitchen organization, 105

About the Author

New York City native **Regina Leeds** has brought order to home and work environments across the country since 1988 when she started her company, Get Organized! by Regina. Currently based in Los Angeles, her clientele run the gamut from studio executives and artists to businesspeople and housewives. Regina regularly travels throughout the United States to assist clients. Her favorite organizing task is unpacking a new home after a move.

Raised a Roman Catholic in Brooklyn, Regina later studied Religious Science for more than 10 years. Following the path of founder Ernest Holmes, she, too, studied the spiritual philosophies of the East. This serendipitously dovetailed with her work as a professional organizer and led to the birth of "Zen organizing."

Regina's first career as a professional actress (she received a Bachelor's degree in theater from Hunter College in Manhattan) has made the transition to teacher and seminar leader an easy one. Regina's credits as a professional actress include national commercials, guest spots on TV, theater roles, and three happy years recurring on *The Young and the Restless*.

In addition to her classes in getting organized, she offers a seminar in collaboration with Feng Shui master Nate Batoon. As a result of the terrorist attacks on September 11, 2001, Regina and Nate are currently raising money for Search and Rescue Dog Teams around the country.

Regina has been featured in national magazines, including *Redbook*, Delta Airlines' *Shuttle Sheet, Bon Appetit, The Utne Reader*, and *New Age Magazine*, among others. She is a resident expert on the Home & Garden Channel at iVillage.com. You can also find Regina on the World Wide Web at www.reginaleeds.com.

Regina's television interviews include *Books on Tour* for the Wisdom Channel with Corinne Edwards, the *Iyanla VanZant Show*, and *Woman to Woman* in Los Angeles.

Regina looks forward to returning home to New York. Hopefully, her Golden Retriever Katie will adapt to the highly aromatic streets of the city. Miss Katie is, by the way, a very organized dog.